The Little Book

of

Buddhist Virtue

The Buddha's teachings on happiness through skillful conduct

by Eric K. Van Horn

Copyright

CreateSpace Independent Publishing Platform
ISBN-13: 978-1530068746
ISBN-10: 1530068746
First Edition 2016 (1)
Revised 2017 (2)

Dedicated to Venerable Ānanda,

Without whose selfless devotion to the Buddha,

Remarkable memory,

And kind heart,

Many of the Buddha's teachings

Would have been lost.

"'The safe and good path to be traveled joyfully' is a term for the Noble Eight Book Path."

The Little Books on Buddhism series:

Book 1: *The Little Book of Buddhist Meditation: Establishing a daily meditation practice*

Book 2: *The Little Book on Buddhist Virtue: The Buddha's teachings on happiness through skillful conduct*

Book 3: *The Little Book of the Life of the Buddha*

Book 4: *The Little Book of Buddhist Wisdom: The Buddha's teachings on the Four Noble Truths, the three marks of existence, causality, and karma*

Book 5: *The Little Book of Buddhist Mindfulness & Concentration*

Book 6: *The Little Book of Buddhist Daily Living: The Discipline for Lay People*

Book 7: *The Little Book of Buddhist Rebirth*

Book 8: *The Little Book of Buddhist Awakening: The Buddha's instructions on attaining enlightenment*

Also by this author:

The Travel Guide to the Buddha's Path

Table of Contents

Preface.. ix

Terminology and Conventions xii

Abbreviations for Pāli Text References xiii

Introduction 1

How to Explain Virtue to a Seven-year-old........................ 4

Generosity 10

The Five Lay Precepts 13

    The First Precept: not killing 14

    The Second Precept: not taking what is not freely
    offered 15

    The Third Precept: abstaining from sexual misconduct17

    The Fourth Precept: abstaining from false speech....... 18

    The Fifth Precept: refraining from the use of intoxicants
    21

Virtue as a Gift.. 23

Virtue in the Four Noble Truths............................. 26

The Wholesome and the Unwholesome 31

Karma 34

    Karma as Intention 34

    Karma as a Complex System 36

    The Probabilistic Nature of Karma 38

    Choice.. 40

    The End of Karma 42

The Ten Perfections 44

  1. Generosity 45

  2. Moral conduct 49

  3. Renunciation 50

  4. Wisdom 54

  5. Energy 56

  6. Patience 59

  7. Honesty 61

  8. Resolve 63

  9. Loving-kindness 66

  10. Equanimity 72

Postscript 78

Appendices 81

  Appendix A - Glossary of Terms 81

  Appendix B - Bibliography 86

Preface

"Thus, Ānanda, the purpose and benefit of wholesome virtuous behavior is non-regret; the purpose and benefit of non-regret is joy; the purpose and benefit of joy is rapture; the purpose and benefit of rapture is tranquility; the purpose and benefit of tranquility is pleasure; the purpose and benefit of pleasure is concentration; the purpose and benefit of concentration is the knowledge and vision of things as they really are; the purpose and benefit of the knowledge and vision of things as they really are is disenchantment and dispassion; and the purpose and benefit of disenchantment and dispassion is the knowledge and vision of liberation. Thus, Ānanda, wholesome virtuous behavior progressively leads to the foremost."
– [AN 10.1]

This is the second volume in the *Little Books on Buddhism* series. In the first Little Book, *The Little Book on Buddhist Meditation*, all of the material comes from the first unit in my book, *The Travel Guide to the Buddha's Path*. But in this Little Book about 80% of the material is new. Indeed, one of the purposes of the Little Books on Buddhism series is to be able to expand on issues that are more lightly covered in the *Travel Guide*.

In the *Travel Guide*, virtue is covered in the section on right view. But here I thought it wise to make it the second topic in the series. In the Buddha's original system of training, virtue is actually the first teaching. It is the foundation of the whole path. I chose to write about "samadhi" – establishing a sense of well-being – first because I think that in the West we are very poor at caring for ourselves. We need to establish an emotionally secure place from which to practice.

But make no mistake about it, in the Buddha's system of training, virtue comes first. He makes this quite clear. And it is unfortunate that through the centuries, establishing a foundation of virtue has been lost in many schools of Buddhism. And if you do not cultivate qualities of virtue, there is almost no point to the rest of the practice. You are likely to just become annoying.

It is equally unfortunate that in the West we have a lot of cultural baggage surrounding the terms "ethics" and "morality," and it is difficult to retrain the mind to think of virtue as a path to happiness. But I hope that in the process of seeing what the Buddha taught that you realize the benefits of a virtuous mind. A mind that is refraining from acts of ethical misconduct like lying, stealing, killing, sexual aggression, etc., is a happier mind than one that is greedy, fearful, full of hatred and anxiety, and delusional.

Of course, virtue includes qualities that go beyond a system of ethics and morality, qualities like patience, wisdom, and equanimity. That also is the aim of this book, to expand what may sound like a moral code to the greater nobility, contentment, and security that come from the life of virtue.

Eric Van Horn
Rio Rancho, New Mexico
14-Feb-2016
nobleeightfoldblog.com

Terminology and Conventions

Because the Buddhist Canon that I use is in the Pāli language, I usually use Pāli terms. However, some Sanskrit Buddhist terms have become common in the English language, and it seems rather affected not to use them. The two most obvious examples are the words "nirvāṇa," which is "nibbāna" in Pāli, and "Dharma," which is "Dhamma" in Pāli. For the most part I use the commonly known terms. But if it seems awkward to have the Pāli terms in quotes or in certain words (like "Dhammacakkappavattana") and use the Sanskrit terms in the main text, I use the Pāli words.

I try to avoid technical terms in the beginning of the guide until you can get used to them. However, if there are terms with which you are unfamiliar, they should be in the glossary in Appendix A.

As per APA style guidelines, book names are italicized (i.e., *Foundations of Buddhism*) and magazine articles and Internet resources are capitalized and quoted (i.e., "The Benefits of Walking Meditation").

Internet Conventions

There are many references to resources that are on the Internet. This is always a problem because hyperlinks are notoriously unreliable. Thus, I have adopted a convention of putting Internet search keywords in the text. For example, a reference to Thich Nhat Hanh's gāthās ("poems") is "thich nhat hanh gathas here and now." If you do an Internet search with your browser, the first item in the search results should be the appropriate resource.

The other case is when an article is sighted. It will look like this:

- [Sayadaw U Silananda, "The Benefits of Walking Meditation"]

Searching on the author's name and the article name should get you to the article. Some names and words use diacritical marks, and you may have to remove them to find the correct resource. For example, for the name "Ṭhānissaro" use the non-diacritical form "Thanissaro."

Abbreviations for Pāli Text References

AN: *Aṅguttara Nikāya, The Numerical Discourses of the Buddha*

Bv: *Buddhavaṃsa, Chronicle of Buddhas*

BvA: *Buddhavaṃsatthakathā*, commentary to the *Buddhavaṃsa*

Cv: *Cullavagga*, the *"smaller book,"* the second volume in the *Khandhaka*, which is the second book of the monastic code (the *Vinaya*)

Dhp: *Dhammapada, The Path of Dhamma*, a collection of 423 verses

DhpA: *Dhammapada-aṭṭhakathā*, commentary to the *Dhammapada*

DN: *Digha Nikāya, The Long Discourses of the Buddha*

Iti: *Itivuttaka, This Was Said* (by the Buddha), Sayings of the Buddha

Ja: *Jātaka Tales*, previous life stories of the Buddha

JaA: *Jātaka-aṭṭhakathā*, commentary on the *Jātaka Tales*

Khp: *Khuddakapāṭha, Short Passages*

MA: *Majjhima Nikāya Aṭṭhakathā*, commentary on *The Middle Length Discourses of the Buddha* (by Buddhaghosa)

MN: *Majjhima Nikāya, The Middle Length Discourses of the Buddha*

Mv: *Mahāvagga*, the first volume in the *Khandhaka*, which is the second book of the monastic code (the *Vinaya*)

Pm: *Pātimokkha, The Code of Monastic Discipline*, the first book of the monastic code (the *Vinaya*)

SN: *Saṃyutta Nikāya, The Connected Discourses of the Buddha*

S Nip: *Sutta Nipāta, The Sutta Collection*, literally, "suttas falling down," a sutta collection in the *Khuddaka Nikāya* consisting mostly of verse

Sv: *Sutta-vibhaṅga: Classification of the Suttas*, the "origin stories" for the Pātimokkha rules

Thag: *Theragāthā: Verses of the Elder Monks*

ThagA: *Theragāthā-aṭṭhakathā*: commentary to the *Theragāthā*

Thig: *Therīgāthā: Verses of the Elder Nuns*

ThigA: *Therīgāthā-aṭṭhakathā*: commentary to the *Therīgāthā*

Ud: *Udana, Exclamations*, the third book of the *Khuddaka Nikāya*

Vin: *Vinaya Pitaka, Basket of Discipline*, the monastic rules for monks and nuns.

Introduction

The English word "morality" and its derivatives suggest a sense of obligation and constraint quite foreign to the Buddhist conception of sīla [morality]; this connotation probably enters from the theistic background to Western ethics. Buddhism, with its non-theistic framework, grounds its ethics, not on the notion of obedience, but on that of harmony. In fact, the commentaries explain the word sīla by another word, "samadhana," meaning "harmony" or "coordination."

- [Bhikkhu Bodhi, *The Noble Eightfold Path*, Chapter IV: Right Speech, Right Action, Right Livelihood]

When I was still early in my study of the Buddha's teachings, I came across the word "virtue." It is not a word that you hear very often. It sounds antiquated and quaint, the sort of thing you throw around when reading about King Arthur and the Knights of the Round Table.

Thich Nhat Hanh says that sometimes words need to be healed. The most egregiously wounded of all words is "love." But I think that the word "virtue" could use some healing of its own.

I went to a retreat once where we were having a discussion about Buddhist morality, and a woman rather angrily said, "Well, I don't want to become a saint!" To this someone else replied, "Do you want to suffer?"

In the West we have this notion of sin, blame, and guilt. If we commit a sin, the results are irredeemable. If we do something wrong, we go to hell. This idea of sin is very problematical in Western Buddhism. It makes conveying the Buddhist sense of virtue very difficult.

There is no notion of sin in Buddhism. There is only cause and effect, actions and their consequences. If your actions are of benefit to yourself and others now and in the future, then continue to do those things. If they are not, then don't. Developing the Buddhist path is a skill, like learning a trade. An apprentice is likely to make errors, and the only "sin" is not learning from them.

Going back to the time of the Buddha, lay followers of the Buddha typically did not meditate. But they did practice the ethical and moral teachings of the Buddha. This means most simply a) the practice of generosity and b) keeping the five lay precepts, although as you will see, the Buddha taught virtue in many ways.

This Little Book begins with one of my favorite discourses of the Buddha, the "Ambalatthika-rahulovada Sutta: Instructions to Rāhula at Mango Stone" [MN 61]. Rāhula was the Buddha's son, and was only seven years old when the Buddha taught him this. Those of you who have children will perhaps appreciate the tender tone of his message and the profundity of the Buddha teaching his own child.

Next is the classic teaching on generosity and the five lay precepts. This is the teaching on virtue with which people are most familiar.

Next comes a particularly favorite teaching of mine. So often we think of morality, ethics, and virtue as a cross to bear. But in this teaching, the Buddha told us that virtue is a gift that we give to the world. It is our empowerment as human beings, a way in which we use our power to make the world a better place. It is how we make a difference.

Then there is a look at the Four Noble Truths. The Four Noble Truths were the topic of the Buddha's first discourse. This discussion will touch lightly on the main points as they pertain to the Noble Eightfold Path, the Buddha's prescription for training. This is mainly to make sure that you understand virtue in the context of the larger training.

Then we look at virtue from another discourse, the "Sammādiṭṭhi Sutta: The Discourse on Right View" [MN 9]. In this discourse, the Buddha's chief disciple Sāriputta discussed the "wholesome and the unwholesome." It is an expanded teaching on the subject of virtue.

This leads to a discussion of karma. It is very important to properly understand what the Buddha said about karma. Even in Buddhist circles karma is often mistaught and misunderstood. This is a core facet of the Buddha's teaching.

And finally we will look at the Ten Perfections, the "pāramīs." This is a fun way to look at Buddhist virtue. In the centuries that followed the Buddha's death, as Buddhism spread throughout Asia, the vast majority of Buddhists not only practiced virtue exclusively, they learned what it means to be virtuous from a literature known as the Jātaka stories. The Jātakas are Buddhist folk tales, similar to Aesop's Fables. They are linked closely to the teaching on the Ten Perfections.

The Buddha's system of training is first and foremost about conduct. He instructed us to cultivate our minds, speech, and actions in a particular direction. In this way we become happier people, more comfortable in the world, more useful to the world, and less likely to cause mischief in the world.

How to Explain Virtue to a Seven-year-old

The Buddha was 29 years old when he left home to become a "samaṇa," a wandering ascetic, or spiritual seeker. He left home on the day that his son Rāhula was born. He left behind his life of wealth and luxury to become homeless and penniless.

Six years later, after almost dying from the severity of his ascetic practices, he gave up those extremes. He adopted a "middle way." He nursed himself back to health, cultivated the "pleasure born of seclusion," and finally broke through to attain an awakening. He became the Buddha.

Some time after that he returned back to his family's home in Sakya. Sakya is on the modern-day border between India and Nepal. During that trip his son Rāhula ordained as a Buddhist monk and followed his father into the holy life.

You can imagine how extraordinary this must have been. Rāhula, of course, did not know his father, and here he was returning from life as a spiritual seeker as the Buddha. It must have been pretty overwhelming for a seven-year-old boy.

They subsequently traveled to the Indian kingdom of Magadha, where they stayed at the Bamboo Forest Monastery. You can visit this place today.

One evening, the Buddha decided to teach his Dharma to Rāhula. This is a pretty unusual event. The Buddha rarely went out of his way to teach. He was constantly being hounded to teach. But on this occasion he sought out his son to teach him the Dharma:

Thus have I heard. On one occasion the Blessed One was living at Rājagaha in the Bamboo Grove, the Squirrels' Sanctuary. Now on that occasion the venerable Rāhula was living at Ambalaṭṭhikā. Then, when it was evening, the Blessed One rose from meditation and went to the venerable Rāhula at Ambalaṭṭhikā. The venerable Rāhula saw the Blessed One coming in the distance and made a seat ready and set out water for washing the feet. The Blessed One sat down on the seat made

ready and washed his feet. The venerable Rāhula paid homage to him and sat down at one side.
- [MN 61.1-2]

Figure: The Bamboo Forest Monastery in modern day Rajgir

The Buddha's teachings, as you may well know, are not simple. To this day even learned monks get many important points wrong. So the issue here is... how could the Buddha teach this vast Dharma to a seven-year-old boy?

His first lesson was about the importance of speaking the truth:

"...Rāhula, when one is not ashamed to tell a deliberate lie, there is no evil, I say, that one would not do. Therefore, Rāhula, you should train thus: 'I will not utter a falsehood even as a joke.'"
- [MN 61.7]

Speaking the truth is held in particularly high regard in Buddhism. In the *Jātakas* (the birth stories of the Buddha), the Buddha-to-be broke all of the precepts at one time or another *except* for the one on speaking the truth:

...it is not just a statement of what is not false but also a steady and even inspiring quality indicative of reliability and excellence of character. It is understood that all bad states in the end arise from a kind of dishonesty. According to popular supposition the

Bodhisatta [Buddha-in-training] *cannot tell a lie. In one rebirth, the Hārita Jātaka (431), the Bodhisatta, after years of ascetic practice, horrifies himself by succumbing repeatedly to lustful passion through an affair with a beautiful woman. When confronted with gossip about this he immediately confesses ... to the king, her husband. As the narrative comments, a Bodhisatta might lapse in other ways but cannot say what is not true."*
- [Sarah Shaw, *The Jātakas: Birth Stories of the Bodhisatta*]

The English language, which does not always map well to Pāli and Sanskrit, in this case provides a similar way to look at the word "true." Something is true if it is a correct statement of fact. But there is also the sense of "being true" and being "honest and true." There is a sense of nobility. And here this maps precisely to the Buddha's first instruction to Rāhula to be honest and true.

Next the Buddha teaches Rāhula about reflecting on his actions before committing them:

"What do you think, Rāhula? What is the purpose of a mirror?"

"For the purpose of reflection, venerable sir."

"So too, Rāhula, an action with the body should be done after repeated reflection; an action by speech should be done after repeated reflection; an action by mind should be done after repeated reflection."
- [MN 61.8]

(In the Buddha's teaching, there are three types of action: actions of the body, actions of speech, and actions of the mind.)

The Buddha went on to say that if, upon reflection, the action will cause harm to him or others, then he should abandon it:

"Rāhula, when you wish to do an action with the body, you should reflect upon that same bodily action thus: 'Would this action that I wish to do with the body lead to my own affliction, or to the affliction of others, or to the affliction of both? Is it an unwholesome bodily action with painful consequences, with painful results?' When you reflect, if you know: 'This action that I wish to do with the body would lead to my own affliction, or to the affliction of others, or to the affliction of both; it is an unwholesome bodily action with painful consequences, with painful results,' then you definitely should not do such an action

6

with the body. But when you reflect, if you know: 'This action that I wish to do with the body would not lead to my own affliction, or to the affliction of others, or to the affliction of both; it is a wholesome bodily action with pleasant consequences, with pleasant results,' then you may do such an action with the body."
- [MN 61.9]

This first case is to contemplate the probable outcome of a bodily action. In the typical Indian philosophical tradition of the day, the Buddha then traced through all of the cases, the next one being while you are in the process of committing a bodily act:

"Also, Rāhula, while you are doing an action with the body, you should reflect upon that same bodily action thus: 'Does this action that I am doing with the body lead to my own affliction, or to the affliction of others, or to the affliction of both?'"
– [MN 61.10]

And the final case, which is when a bodily action has already happened:

"Also, Rāhula, after you have done an action with the body, you should reflect upon that same bodily action thus: 'Did this action that I did with the body lead to my own affliction, or to the affliction of others, or to the affliction of both?'"
– [MN 61.11]

The Buddha continued to cover speech and mental actions (thoughts) in the same way. Thus we have nine cases: bodily acts in the past, present and future, acts of speech in the past, present and future, and mental actions in the past, present and future.

(Those of you who are mathematically oriented will recognize this as a two-dimensional matrix, with past-present-future on one dimension, and bodily actions-speech-mental actions as the other. This is how cases in Indian philosophy were asserted. However they did not have the notion of a matrix at that time. In what may seem curious to us they used the notion of a wheel instead. The nine cases here would have made up the nine spokes of the wheel. Since those nine cases make up all of the possible cases the wheel was said to be "complete.")

The Buddha then summarized in this way:

"Rāhula, whatever recluses and brahmins in the past purified their bodily action, their verbal action, and their mental action, all did so by repeatedly reflecting thus. Whatever recluses and brahmins in the future will purify their bodily action, their verbal action, and their mental action, all will do so by repeatedly reflecting thus. Whatever recluses and brahmins in the present are purifying their bodily action, their verbal action, and their mental action, all are doing so by repeatedly reflecting thus. Therefore, Rāhula, you should train thus: 'We will purify our bodily action, our verbal action, and our mental action by repeatedly reflecting upon them.'"
- [MN 61.18]

In teaching Rāhula to look at his past actions, he used reflection and past experiences and past actions as a learning tool. There is no sense of guilt or shame. Now, of course, unskillful actions can cause shame and unhappiness. In fact that is one of the points of this teaching. The more virtue one has, the happier one is likely to be. This is a very important point. Ethical behavior is part of the path to greater happiness.

On the other hand, wallowing in guilt and shame about past behavior is pointless. So in rather clinical fashion the Buddha advised us to remember the sense of guilt or shame, and then move past that, to learn from our mistakes, and to act more skillfully in the future. In this way we can avoid the guilt and shame that resulted from our unskillful behavior.

Another important point is that the action "have pleasant consequences" for yourself and others. I think that in the West we are particularly bad at taking care of ourselves. It is a difficult case to make that when we take care of ourselves, we are also taking care of the people around us. But that is a key point in all of the Buddha's teaching. We can do a lot of good by developing a skillful, healthy mind. Conversely, we do a lot of mischief by not cultivating and training our minds.

There is an iconic story that the Buddha told to illustrate this point. It is the "Sedaka Sutta: The Bamboo Acrobat" [AN 47.19]. It begins with a master acrobat telling his student how they will do a trick:

"Bhikkhus, once in the past an acrobat set up his bamboo pole and addressed his apprentice Medakathālikā thus: 'Come, dear

Medakathālikā, climb the bamboo pole and stand on my shoulders.'

Having replied, 'Yes, teacher,' the apprentice Medakathālikā climbed up the bamboo pole and stood on the teacher's shoulders.

The acrobat then said to the apprentice Medakathālikā: 'You protect me, dear Medakathālikā, and I'll protect you. Thus guarded by one another, protected by one another, we'll display our skills, collect our fee, and get down safely from the bamboo pole.'

When this was said, the apprentice Medakathālikā replied: 'That's not the "way to do it, teacher. You protect yourself, teacher, and I'll protect myself. Thus, each self-guarded and self-protected, we'll display our skills, collect our fee, and get down safely from the bamboo pole.'"
- [SN 47.19]

The Buddha ended this discourse by summarizing in this way:

"'I will protect myself,' bhikkhus: thus should the establishments of mindfulness be practised. 'I will protect others,' bhikkhus: thus should the establishments of mindfulness be practised. Protecting oneself, bhikkhus, one protects others; protecting others, one protects oneself."

I think that one of the greatest misunderstandings about the Buddha's teachings is that they are "self-centered," that they only focus on individual liberation. But that greatly underestimates the harm that we do because of our unskillfulness. By cultivating skill and wisdom, we are of immensely more value to the world around us.

The Buddha's instructions to his son Rāhula are elegantly simple. Be truthful, and reflect on your actions. This includes what you think as well as what you say and do. Train yourself to act only when it is of benefit to yourself and others, now and in the future.

Generosity

"If beings knew, as I know, the results of giving and sharing, they would not eat without having given, nor would the stain of miserliness overcome their minds. Even if it were their last bite, their last mouthful, they would not eat without having shared, if there were someone to receive their gift. But because beings do not know, as I know, the results of giving and sharing, they eat without having given. The stain of miserliness overcomes their minds."
- [Iti 1.26]

The foundation of the Buddha's teachings is generosity. It is the ground upon which the entire path lays.

In Buddhist countries like Thailand, the first thing that children learn is the practice of generosity. Monks go on daily alms rounds, and the children put food into the monks' bowls. This is the only food that the monks will get that day; they are not even allowed to store food. So the children are doing something very important. And because monks are so revered in those countries, the children get a great deal of joy from the act of giving.

Generosity is both the beginning and the end of the path. The cause of our dukkha is craving. Craving is something we want. Generosity is something we give. It is the perfect antidote for craving.

If you are ever feeling sad or depressed, a very good antidote is to do something for someone else. When we are depressed, it is like being in an emotional phone booth. We are self-absorbed; everything seems tight and constricted. But when you do something for someone else, it forces you outside of yourself. It is a way to open up the heart.

Joseph Goldstein says that we often think of things to do for other people, but we hardly ever follow through on them. So when you think of something generous to do, do it. Turn generosity into a good habit.

Unfortunately generosity is something that we often feel that we have to do, not something we want to do. We must train ourselves to feel the joy that comes from generosity. When you do something generous, don't just skip over the joy and satisfaction. Open up to it.

In Pāli there are two closely related words about generosity. The most commonly heard one is "dana" (pronounced like the name "Donna"). "Dana" literally means "the act of giving." The other related word is "caga." "Caga" is a "heart bent on giving."

A common misunderstanding about generosity is that it is about giving money or things. Traditionally in Buddhism, the most generous act is sharing the teachings. This is the generosity provided by monks and nuns. They don't have any material possessions, but what they give is the teachings and their effort in cultivating the path. This is important to remember when you are meditating. As the Buddha said, the best way to meditate is for yourself and others. When you are meditating, it is a gift of generosity. You are cultivating your mind so that you can cause less mischief and do more good.

"...there are these four kinds of persons found existing in the world. What four? One who is practicing neither for his own welfare nor for the welfare of others; one who is practicing for the welfare of others but not for his own welfare; one who is practicing for his own welfare but not for the welfare of others; and one who is practicing both for his own welfare and for the welfare of others.

"...The person practicing both for his own welfare and for the welfare of others is the foremost, the best, the preeminent, the supreme, and the finest of these four persons."
- [AN 4.95]

So when you are meditating it is a gift of generosity. You are cultivating your mind so that you can cause less mischief and do more good.

One of the greatest ways that you can be generous is with your attention. When you are talking with someone, give them your full attention. Be aware of all the invisible people in the world, like the person who bags your groceries or cleans your motel room. I am often amazed at how uncomfortable this makes some people feel. They are so used to being invisible that if you pay them common courtesy they don't know how to respond. Be on a mission to give the gift of your full attention and respect to everyone.

There is also a wisdom aspect to generosity. As the Buddha taught, the most important aspect of karma is our intention:

"Intention, I tell you, is karma. Intending, one does karma by way of body, speech and mind."

- [AN 6.63]

We want to give with a full and open heart, of course. This is "caga." But we should also use some discernment. There are charities that are not very effective. They give exorbitant salaries to their managers. And you don't want to give money to people who will just misuse it, like addicts or chronic gamblers.

There will be times when you do something with the best of intentions and then later realize it was unskillful. That is not a problem. When you did it, you did it with the wisest intentions that you could muster at the time. That is all we can do. But then learn from that. The Buddhist path is all about learning. We learn, and that is how we develop and progress. As Larry Rosenberg says, in Buddhism, we learn our way out of suffering.

In Buddhist countries the greatest form of giving for lay people is to the monks and nuns. This brings more "merit." (Of course there are some quite mischievous monks, so that is no guarantee, either.)

Another quality we are trying to cultivate is an internal motivation with an internal result. Of course, people like to be thanked for their gifts. But it is useful to learn to detach yourself from any result. I once read about a practice where when you do something generous you make it a point not to tell anyone about it. It is amazing how difficult this can be. If we do something nice, we want people to know about it. But it is also a very good practice to keep it to yourself. Learn to make your own sense of satisfaction the reward. Try it and see what the results are.

Having said that, in Buddhist countries it is a tradition to recognize people for their gifts. Temples have the names of the benefactors carved on them. The 19th century engineer James Prinsep was able to decipher an ancient Indian script by recognizing that the writing on ancient temples was a donor list [Charles Allen, *The Search for the Buddha*]. It is perfectly proper and perfectly within the Buddhist tradition to be recognized for your generosity and to feel joy and happiness in that generosity. Buddhist organizations should make it a practice to acknowledge people for their generosity.

These are all ways in which we learn skillful giving, and we cultivate the joy of generosity.

The Five Lay Precepts

Traditionally when a lay person formally becomes a Buddhist they do two things. First, they take refuge in the Three Jewels: the Buddha, the Dharma, and the Saṇgha (specifically the monastic Saṇgha and the noble Saṇgha). The Three Jewels are a safe haven, like a good harbor that shields ships from a storm.

The other thing you do to become a Buddhist is to take the five precepts.

Buddhism is creed-less. To formally become a Buddhist, you do not have to agree to believe anything. (Although you won't get very far if you do not believe that your actions have results.) But you do have to agree to behave in a certain way. The word for this is "orthopraxy." An "orthodoxy" is a system of belief; an "orthopraxy" is a system of conduct.

The principle behind the five precepts is that, as the Buddha says, wholesome actions lead to wholesome results and unwholesome actions lead to unwholesome results. The precepts give a more precise definition of what wholesome actions are.

There are two reasons why the precepts cause problems for Westerners. The first comes from our Judeo-Christian heritage. We are afraid that if we break a precept we are going to go to hell. That is a stark way to put it, but that cultural conditioning is usually lurking in the background.

When I was in India the person who led the trip wanted everyone to take the precepts. There was one woman who really had trouble with that. She kept using the word "vow" when discussing the precepts. She came from a Catholic background where a vow is something that you cannot break under any circumstances. Once you break a vow, you are defeated, and there is no way to undo the damage.

But that is not the spirit of the precepts. Thich Nhat Hanh uses the term "trainings" rather than "precepts." That is a better way to describe the principle. Again, we are cultivating and developing our minds. The precepts give us a sense of direction. Thich Nhat Hanh compares the "trainings" to the North Star. When you follow the North Star you don't expect to get to the North Star, you expect to go north. The precepts are a way for us to head north.

So we start with the precepts as objectives. When we break one, we reflect on our actions, and see if we can do better the next time. We contemplate how to do that; we come up with a strategy. We turn it into a problem-solving exercise.

The other problem Westerners tend to have is guilt about what they have done in the past. Misunderstandings about karma can feed that. But what has happened has happened. There is no point in feeling guilty about the past. In fact, guilt can keep us from moving forward. What matters are the choices we make now and in the future. We want to nurture our mental development in a certain way, a way that is more skillful. We have decided to run a marathon, but we have never run more than a 100 feet. So we have some work to do. But if you spend all your time lamenting that you have never run in the past, it is a complete waste of time.

The First Precept: not killing

Pāṇātipātā veramaṇī sikkhāpadaṃ samādiyāmi.
I undertake the training rule to abstain from killing.

The canonical definition of killing extends to living beings that have "breath and consciousness." This includes people and all animal life, including insects, but not plant life. The Pāli word for "killing" also implies more generally "harming." Thus this first precept is also sometimes called "basic non-harming."

This precept is particularly difficult to keep. Life feeds on life, and we are part of that system. It is nearly impossible to go through a normal day without doing something that harms or even kills. In our modern world where we are usually unaware of the collateral damage of our actions, it is particularly difficult.

In the monastic code the Buddha put the emphasis on one's intention. So if one does not intend to harm, there is no offense. There is a difference between stepping on an ant accidentally and doing it intentionally. More fundamentally it is the quality of our heart and mind that is most important.

The question often comes up as to whether eating meat breaks the first precept. That is a difficult one, especially because we are so disconnected from our food sources.

It may surprise you to know that in southern Buddhism, monks and nuns are not forbidden to eat meat. This was also true at the time of the Buddha. This requires a little context. Because monks and nuns eat alms food, they accept all that is given. It is an act of gratitude. Thus, it has less to do with what one eats than accepting the generosity of the people who are giving you food. In some cases, the people who are feeding you have very little themselves, and it would be unkind to refuse what they give.

There is an extended set of monastic rules called the "dhutanga" ("ascetic practices") that monks and nuns may undertake, and these include adhering to a vegetarian diet. But refraining from eating meat is not in the standard monastic code.

Having said that, over time it has become a convention to only give vegetarian food to monks and nuns. In eastern Buddhism (China, Japan, Korea, and Viet Nam), vegetarianism is the rule. Mahāyāna Buddhists take the Bodhisattva vows that forbid the eating of meat. In Tibet, where it is nearly impossible to grow anything, the eating of meat is the norm.

However, we live in an era where being a vegetarian is easy. There are so many options that do not include meat. Conversely, the raising and killing of animals creates a lot of suffering. It is extremely destructive to the environment, and vegetarian diets are usually healthier. So if you are not a vegetarian, you might consider making a difference in this way.

The Second Precept: not taking what is not freely offered

Adinnādānā veramaṇī sikkhāpadaṃ samādiyāmi
I undertake the training rule to abstain from taking what is not given.

The precept on stealing is usually phrased as shown above, although it is also common to say, "I undertake the training rule to abstain from taking what is not freely given." This makes it clear that you should avoid even subtle forms of coercion.

The exact phrasing of the precept on stealing comes from Sakyan civil law. Sakya was the Buddha's home country. And there is a story in the Canon that demonstrates this law. It occurs in several places, including the Vinaya, the monastic code.

Six Sakyan princes were inspired to "go forth" and become disciples of the Buddha. They left Sakya with their barber Upāli. At a certain point in their journey they removed their princely clothes and jewelry and gave them to Upāli with the expectation that he would take them back to Sakya with him.

However, Upāli reasoned, "the Sakyans are a fierce people. They will think that I have murdered the youths, and they might kill me." So Upāli, too, decided to go forth and ordain as a monk. But before he set off, he took the fine things and hanged them from a tree, saying, "Let him who finds it take it as a gift." By saying this, anyone who took these things would not be guilty of stealing because he had "freely offered them" [Vin ii.182].

(The story has an even happier ending. Upāli became enlightened and a highly revered monk, "foremost in knowledge of the [monastic code]" – [AN 1.14.228].)

The monastic code devotes a lot of attention to subtle coercion. Monks and nuns are not allowed to ask for anything except water. This may seem a little extreme, but the Buddha was very sensitive to how religious people abuse their power and authority. He went to great lengths to keep the monastic Saṅgha "pure." Monks and nuns are not allowed to make their preferences known even in subtle ways.

This is an important point. Sadly, there is as much abuse in Buddhism as in any other religion. There are many instances of Buddhist leaders taking advantage of their students, materially and sexually. Some of the most famous are Richard Baker, who was Shunryu Suzuki's heir at the San Francisco Zen Center, Chogyam Trungpa, who was a sexual predator, heavy drinker and smoker, and more recently Joshu Sazaki who was "groping and sexually harassing female students for decades," according to the New York Times. Sazaki even tried to break up the marriage of one of his students, and encouraged him to have an affair.

The writer Natalie Goldberg wrote a book called *The Great Failure: My Unexpected Path to Truth* about discovering that her teacher Dainin Katagiri sexually abused his students for decades.

One of the purposes of the monastic code is to protect both the Saṅgha and the laity.

The goal of the Buddha's teachings is to reduce suffering, to do good when possible, and to do so with love, compassion, and wisdom. So this precept is very important. We are trying to be happy with what we have.

As with the first precept, this is almost impossible to keep. By our very existence we take what is not freely offered. The land and the animals on which our lives depend do not freely offer what we take. So we take as little as possible. We treat what we take as a sacred trust. Everything that we use has a cost associated with it, and the less we take, the farther north we get.

The Third Precept: abstaining from sexual misconduct

Kāmesumicchācāra veramaṇī sikkhāpadaṃ samādiyāmi.
I undertake the training rule to avoid sensual misconduct.

(In Pāli the same word is used for "sensual" and "sexual.")

The Buddha devoted a lot of attention to the dangers of sexual energy. Anyone who is a true Dharma follower cannot rationalize the abuses of people like Richard Baker, Chogyam Trungpa, Joshu Sazaki and Dainin Katagiri. It is not possible to call people like these followers of the Buddha's teaching.

I have heard many rationalizations about sexual abuse by teachers. One person I knew rationalized sex abuse by saying that the "precepts are empty." "Emptiness" is sometimes used as a way to excuse atrocious behavior. This is a complete misrepresentation of those teachings. Emptiness is not nihilism. The universe is a realm of causes and conditions. The law of karma is ethically based, and it is the quality of our intentions that determines the karmic results of our actions. Thus, to rationalize unethical behavior based on "emptiness" is something diametrically opposed to the Dharma.

When this precept is violated, a human being is violated. The potential damage is extremely high. I live in New Mexico where one in three women on Navajo Reservations have been raped or are victims of attempted rape. In the United States a woman's chance of being a victim of rape or attempted rape is one in five. Think about that the next time that you walk down the street. Every fifth woman you see will be a victim of sexual assault.

And as we have just seen, being a practicing Buddhist is no guarantee of safety, even from your teacher.

While there are women who violate this precept, it is mainly men who do. This is where the precepts as a gift are particularly powerful. Using your sexual energy in a responsible and respectful way is a gift that men can give to women. It is the gift of safety. It is a way to be a son, a brother, and a father to women, and not a threat.

For women who use their sexual energy in a way that is ultimately demeaning, like promiscuity or prostitution, have respect for yourself. Show yourself the same love, compassion, and wisdom you have for your dearest friend.

The Fourth Precept: abstaining from false speech

Musāvādā veramaṇī sikkhāpadaṃ samādiyāmi.
I undertake the training rule to abstain from false speech.

What I am about to explain is how the precept on speech is usually explained. However, before I go into that description, let me make a fine point.

The precept on speech only refers to lying. However, elsewhere the Buddha taught – many times – about right speech. Right speech has four aspects to it, one of which is lying. However, the Buddha recognized that there may be extreme cases in which the other forms of wrong speech may be necessary, thus the precept only refers to lying.

An example of one of the types of wrong speech that may be necessary is harsh speech. The Buddha was sometimes quite harsh in his treatment of his monks and nuns. But this was because he was "firing for effect." He was coming down on them for their own welfare out of compassion. But be very, very careful if you try and do this yourself.

There are four different types of wrong speech:

And what, bhikkhus, is wrong speech? False speech, malicious speech, harsh speech, and gossip: this is wrong speech.
- [MN 117.19]

And right speech:

And what, bhikkhus, is right speech... partaking of merit, ripening in the acquisitions? Abstinence from false speech, abstinence from malicious speech, abstinence from harsh speech, abstinence from gossip: this is right speech.
- [MN 117.19]

We probably cause more problems with speech than with anything else we do. Whoever made up that saying about "sticks and stones" was completely off the mark. Countries go to war because of unskillful speech. Marriages break up. Fights start. People can be terribly hurt by unskillful speech. I am pretty sure that someone has said something to you that has been extremely painful. I am also guessing that you have said something that hurt someone else. I know I have.

Of all the Buddha's teachings on ethics and morality, I think that the ones on speech are the hardest to master. We are so used to having words fly out of our mouths without any thought or care. Some years ago I was in a Zen group, and one week our teacher told us to pick one precept on which to work especially diligently. Everyone in the group except one chose speech, just because it is so challenging.

There are four different types of wrong speech in Buddhism:

1. **Being deceitful** - This does not just mean "not lying." People can say something that is factually true, but it can still be deceitful. It can also have no benefit, and cause harm.
2. **Harsh speech** (speaking abusively) - This type of speech is meant to hurt someone.
3. **Malicious speech** (speech that "causes discord in the community") - This would include spreading ill will, talking behind someone's back, etc. Fox News is the poster child for this type of wrong speech.
4. **Idle speech** (gossip) – This is talking without any positive purpose or intent.

This does not mean that you have to sugar coat everything you say. The Buddha was from the warrior class, and he was not shy about reprimanding misbehaving monks. The difference is that he did it without malice or ill will. He did it out of compassion, right intention. That is a very tricky thing, to be able to do that. It is useful to think about our speech as having some positive result, now or in the future, not necessarily that it is pleasant.

In the "Abhayarājakumāra Sutta: To Prince Abhaya" [MN 58], the Buddha gave a different and more detailed teaching on right speech.

"So too, prince, such speech as the Tathāgata knows to be untrue, incorrect, and unbeneficial, and which is also unwelcome and disagreeable to others: such speech the Tathāgata does not utter. Such speech as the Tathāgata knows to be true and correct

but unbeneficial, and which is also unwelcome and disagreeable to others: such speech the Tathāgata does not utter. Such speech as the Tathāgata knows to be true, correct, and beneficial, but which is unwelcome and disagreeable to others: the Tathāgata knows the time to use such speech. Such speech as the Tathāgata knows to be untrue, incorrect, and unbeneficial, but which is welcome and agreeable to others: such speech the Tathāgata does not utter. Such speech as the Tathāgata knows to be true and correct but unbeneficial, and which is welcome and agreeable to others: such speech the Tathāgata does not utter. Such speech as the Tathāgata knows to be true, correct, and beneficial, and which is welcome and agreeable to others: the Tathāgata knows the time to use such speech. Why is that? Because the Tathāgata has compassion for beings."
- [MN 58.8]

Here the Buddha used a different way to determine whether or not something is right speech.

The first criterion is, is it true and correct?

The second criterion is, is it beneficial?

The third criterion is, is it welcome and agreeable?

In order to be right speech, it must be true and correct. It must also be beneficial. However, if the first two criteria are true, then the third criteria may or may not be true. Thus speech that is true and correct and beneficial, can either be welcome and agreeable or not. It doesn't have to be easy to hear.

Conversely, if it is not beneficial, even if it is true and correct, and either welcome or not, there is no point in speaking. In other words, don't waste your breath.

Elsewhere, the Buddha gave a somewhat different formulation:

"Bhikkhus, there are these five courses of speech that others may use when they address you: their speech may be timely or untimely, true or untrue, gentle or harsh, connected with good or with harm, spoken with a mind of loving-kindness or with inner hate."
- [MN 21.11]

Here he added two other factors. One is timeliness. Is this the right time to say something, even if it is true and beneficial? There is a saying in business management, "Praise in public; criticize in private."

That is a good rule. Someone may be very angry or upset. This may not be the time to say certain things to them.

The other factor the Buddha added is a recurring theme in his teaching, and that is the intention behind the action. Did it come from a mind of "loving-kindness or with inner hate?"

You may see by now that one of the characteristics of the Buddha's teaching is how practical it is. That doesn't make it easy. Keeping all this in mind while speaking requires considerable training. Our habits when it comes to speech are deeply ingrained. On the other hand, this isn't rocket science. We "keep in mind" what right speech is, and we examine the consequences of our actions. It is always a case of cause and effect. And that is how we learn our way into greater skill, greater happiness, and greater usefulness as human beings.

The Fifth Precept: refraining from the use of intoxicants

Surā meraya majja pamādaṭṭhānā veramaṇī sikkhāpadaṃ samādiyāmi.
I undertake the training rule to abstain from the use of intoxicants to the point of heedlessness.

The fifth precept causes a lot of consternation in the West, and different people deal with it in different ways.

There is nothing inherently wrong with using intoxicants. The problem is that they tend to lead to breaking one of the other precepts. As this precept says, it is a problem of heedlessness. I never did anything under the influence of intoxicants that I was proud of. The converse is, sadly, true. I regret many things I did while intoxicated. So I think that is all pretty straightforward.

I once sat on a grand jury, and about 11 out of every 10 cases we heard involved alcohol or drugs. This included a particularly disturbing case where a police officer was murdered. The killers had just stolen $100 from a convenience store.

The literal meaning of this precept is abstinence. A lot of people say to that, well, what is the harm in a single glass of wine? Thich Nhat Hanh says to that, well, if you skip the first glass, then you never get to the third one. That is the traditional, hard-line response. In Buddhist countries like Thailand, alcohol is not even available, although that is changing with Western tourism. There are also the inevitable loopholes.

However, in some of the Buddha's discourses, there are only the first four precepts, so this one was a later addition. (There is a rather amusing story about a drunken monk that led to this precept.) That does not make it any less important; it is just worth noting. And a somewhat different interpretation is that the fifth precept only applies to intoxication and not to simple consumption.

I cannot answer all of those questions for you. Clearly, if you choose to consume intoxicants, you must be careful about what you do. This applies particularly in our modern world where email and social media make it so easy to engage in wrong conduct. The simplest route is complete abstinence. But at least be wary of your actions if you have consumed an intoxicant.

Virtue as a Gift

This is my favorite formulation of virtue in the Pāli Canon. It occurs in the *Aṅguttara Nikāya*. Here the Buddha teaches the precepts as a gift that we give to the world:

"There are, bhikkhus, these five gifts, great gifts, primal, of long standing, traditional, ancient, unadulterated and never before adulterated, which are not being adulterated and will not be adulterated, not repudiated by wise ascetics and brahmins. What five?

"Here, a noble disciple, having abandoned the destruction of life, abstains from the destruction of life. By abstaining from the destruction of life, the noble disciple gives to an immeasurable number of beings freedom from fear, enmity, and affliction. He himself in turn enjoys immeasurable freedom from fear, enmity, and affliction. This is the first gift, a great gift, primal, of long standing, traditional, ancient, unadulterated and never before adulterated, which is not being adulterated and will not be adulterated, not repudiated by wise ascetics and brahmins."
- [AN 8.39]

(The Buddha went on to enumerate the other four precepts.)

This is another doorway to virtue. Now the practice of ethics, morality, and virtue is not a burden, or something where we suffer terrible consequences if we don't "follow the rules." It is a gift that we give to the world. By not killing we give the gift of life, we give "immeasurable beings freedom from fear, enmity, and affliction." In turn we enjoy "immeasurable freedom from fear, enmity, and affliction." This is a gift that is "long standing, traditional, ancient, unadulterated and never before adulterated":

The Aṅguttara Nikāya mentions five great gifts which have been held in high esteem by noble-minded [people] from ancient times (A.iv,246). Their value was not doubted in ancient times, it is not doubted at present, nor will it be doubted in the future. The wise recluses and brahmins had the highest respect for them. These great givings comprise the meticulous observance of the Five Precepts. By doing so one gives fearlessness, love and benevolence to all beings. If one human being can give security and freedom from fear to others by his behavior, that is the highest form of dana one can give, not only to mankind, but to all living beings.

- [Lily de Silva, "Giving in the Pāli Canon"]

Here again we see that dana – generosity – is not about writing a check. It is about developing our minds so that we give the gift of moral conduct.

Often in the world we feel helpless in the face of so much turmoil, pain, and suffering. The precepts are a very personal way in which we can make a difference.

We meet life where it touches us, and in those moments we make a difference, even if it is just in the simple act of fully acknowledging the person who is cleaning our motel room.

You may have noticed that thus far there is nothing particularly Buddhist about anything we have discussed. To be sure there will be times when that is not true. But in the discussion of "right conduct" you could come from almost any background, religious or not.

The author of the following passage was Loren Eiseley, who was famously "not of any religion." The story is called "Starfish":

Once upon a time, there was a wise man who used to go to the ocean to do his writing. He had a habit of walking on the beach before he began his work.

One day, as he was walking along the shore, he looked down the beach and saw a human figure moving like a dancer. He smiled to himself at the thought of someone who would dance to the day, and so, he walked faster to catch up.

As he got closer, he noticed that the figure was that of a young man, and that what he was doing was not dancing at all. The young man was reaching down to the shore, picking up small objects, and throwing them into the ocean.

He came closer still and called out "Good morning! May I ask what it is that you are doing?"

The young man paused, looked up, and replied "Throwing starfish into the ocean."

"I must ask, then, why are you throwing starfish into the ocean?" asked the somewhat startled wise man.

To this, the young man replied, "The sun is up and the tide is going out. If I don't throw them in, they'll die."

Upon hearing this, the wise man commented, "But, young man, do you not realize that there are miles and miles of beach and there are starfish all along every mile? You can't possibly make a difference!"

At this, the young man bent down, picked up yet another starfish, and threw it into the ocean. As it met the water, he said, "It made a difference for that one."

- [Loren Eiseley, *The Unexpected Universe*]

Virtue in the Four Noble Truths

After the Buddha attained his awakening, he went in search of companions with whom he had practiced for a long time. They had abandoned him when he gave up the ascetic practices, thinking that he had "gone soft." But now that the Buddha was, well, the Buddha, he thought that he might be able to teach them what he had found.

Thus, the Buddha gave his very first discourse, the "Dhammacakkappavattana Sutta: The Turning of the Wheel of the Dhamma" [SN 56.11]. In this discourse the Buddha taught the Four Noble Truths, his most fundamental teaching.

In the Four Noble Truths, the Buddha laid out the path to awakening, the Noble Eightfold Path. The eight folds are:

1. Right view
2. Right intention
3. Right speech
4. Right action
5. Right livelihood
6. Right effort
7. Right mindfulness
8. Right concentration

Folds three, four and five may look suspiciously familiar. In fact, they are called the "virtue division" of the Noble Eightfold Path. Thus, from the very beginning the Buddha pointed out the importance of virtuous behavior.

As he often did, the Buddha formulated virtue here in a particular way that was appropriate to the situation. Here speech is separated out from "right action." And right livelihood does not usually appear in the formulation of virtue. It is especially interesting that he calls out right livelihood to a group of samaṇas, who were essentially monks. (In the first discourse, technically speaking there were no monks yet.) Of course, through the ages plenty of religious people have used their status for personal gain, and the aim here is "right" livelihood, meaning that one practices in a true and noble way.

Speech and right action are covered elsewhere, but it is worth saying something about right livelihood:

"And what, bhikkhus, is wrong livelihood? Scheming, talking, hinting, belittling, pursuing gain with gain: this is wrong livelihood."
- [MN 117.29]

Here the Buddha pointed to specific types of unethical behavior. Elsewhere he gave precise rules for livelihoods that are considered wrong:

"A lay follower should not engage in five types of business. Which five? Business in weapons, business in human beings, business in meat, business in intoxicants, and business in poison."
- [AN 5.177]

And any kind of livelihood that breaks one of the other ethical principles is suspect as well.

Be wary of confusing right livelihood with political correctness. I went to a retreat once where I wrote down on the registration form that I was a software engineer. I was treated to a lengthy, public berating by a prominent meditation teacher about the evils of corporations. I never said a word. She read my occupation from a sheet of paper and off she went.

I was a psychology major in college, and I was originally trained as a community organizer. I worked for several years in social service organizations. I finally left that career under troubling circumstances that involved corrupt administrators and unethical behavior. I also dealt with widespread incompetence. I eventually came to believe that most social service organizations are ineffective, and most therapists do little to help their clients.

I spent most of my life as a software engineer working for a company in the field of medical informatics. The purpose of the company was to develop technology for improving medical care. Although obviously we had to make money to stay in business, the primary goal was not to make a profit. I used to jokingly refer to it as "a non-profit corporation." While that company was ultimately not very successful, the people who worked there were very dedicated to what we were doing.

Being ineffective does not necessarily make you guilty of wrong livelihood, but be careful about making snap judgments based on a particular occupation. Even the Dalai Lama said once that if a psychotherapist cannot help a large majority of clients (I think he said "80%"), they should find another line of work. It is not enough to have a good sounding job.

It is also unfortunate that in the West we have invented institutions of *Dharma for hire,* where lay people teach the Dharma, after which the famous "dana talk" is given. They expect to be paid. Never mind that most of them have never been trained in a formal way or read so much as a single volume of the Pāli Canon. The Buddha's teachings are supposed to be offered freely. And "free" means "free," not "free" as in I will pretend to give them for free and then give a self-serving talk about how you ought to give me money.

No less an illustrious person than the Dalai Lama has commented on the danger inherent in charging for Dharma teachings:

Say one sets up a Buddhist center, and the center becomes merely a way of making a living. This is truly dangerous. Similarly, if a center becomes solely a vehicle for raising money, that too is not good. This reminds me of an autobiography of a Nyingma lama from Kongpo called Tselé Natsok Rangdröl. He was a monk and a great practitioner. In the autobiography, he mentions that in Tibet, the main way of getting from one place to another place was by riding a horse. He writes that, from a very young age, he decided to give up mounting horses out of compassion for the animals. He would always walk from place to place. Later on, he also gave up eating meat. Because he was a lama with a title, wherever he went many people—devotees— made offerings to him. He felt that in some sense, he was becoming a merchant of spiritual teaching. Thus he made a point of not accepting any offerings for the teachings that he gave. He set a truly remarkable example.

Several years ago, I began refusing any offering for the teachings I give. In the past, it had been customary to make offerings to me at the conclusion of a teaching, but I do not need any money for myself — I have nothing to spend it on. Previously, I would divide the offering up among various deserving projects and causes. When I did that, I would sometimes forget important projects, and people would feel left out and disappointed, thinking, "Oh, the Dalai Lama didn't give any to us, he gave it to them." It was becoming a chore, an unnecessary responsibility, and a headache, worrying about who should get the money. Thus I made it clear that I don't want to receive any offering and thereby end up with this extra burden. Instead the organizers should endeavor to keep the price of the tickets down so that more people can afford to benefit from these teachings. If people want to donate to different causes, they don't have to do it through me.

- [Dalai Lama, *The Middle Way: Faith Grounded in Reason by the Dalai Lama*]

In contrast, one of the most important people in Buddhist history is Anāthapiṇḍika. He was a wealthy businessperson, a great benefactor, and he attained the fruit of stream entry (the first stage of awakening). He is portrayed as a wise, skillful, and compassionate person, and the very embodiment of generosity. It is clear from the descriptions of Anāthapiṇḍika that he was wealthy because he was very skillful in business. There is no negative connotation to his wealth. In fact, wealth is often described as being the fruit of generosity. Money is never described directly or implicitly as being a bad thing.

Likewise, the Buddha often used craftsmanship and trade in his similes for practice. In Indian cities of the Buddha's time there were concentric bands to the city. The central band was where the government was. One of the outer bands was where the craftspeople worked. The Buddha must have spent many hours walking around these shops, watching the various craftsmen at work. In his teaching the wealth and prosperity that come from being a good businessperson or skilled craftsman is seen as a fruit of one's hard work and skill. And people who prosper from their hard work and skill can take care of their families, their friends, and the people around them. They can support charitable causes. They can do a lot of good.

In medieval China, it was common for lay Buddhists to live relatively normal lives, raising families and working in business or crafts. They lived frugally so that when their children were of age they could retire and devote the rest of their lives to their Buddhist practice. Throughout Buddhist history middle class merchants have been the heart of the support for Buddhism.

There is a great deal that you can learn from a career, and from the discipline of learning skills. In the "Mangala Sutta: The Highest Blessings" [Khp 5] one of the blessings is the satisfaction that comes from craftsmanship:

Accomplished in learning and craftsman's skills,
With discipline, highly trained...

That discipline can be transferred to practicing the Dharma. That is immensely valuable in this very challenging practice.

This is a favorite topic of mine because of how much I learned from my career as a software engineer. I discovered computers rather late in life. I was about 28, and at the time I was incredibly undisciplined. But computers are notoriously unsympathetic to our neuroses. It took a long time and at times it was quite challenging, but eventually I learned to have a little more patience and humility. The computer really didn't care about my opinions.

Meditation and Buddhist practice as a whole is a skill and a craft, and you can gain a lot from learning a conventional skill and transferring those lessons to your practice. Ajahn Viradhammo says this:

In monasticism, we are craftspeople, not artists. The work we do is not spectacular... It's about quietly plying one's craft.

...How do you learn something new? Perhaps you're asked to throw a pot and you've never done it before. You can't lift the clay, or it keeps getting floppy. Eventually, you learn to apply an even pressure, and the clay starts to rise...

It's the same with the craft of the heart... something like patience is not something you get by one tremendous insight. You have various insights to it, but then the craft is remembering and training. These incremental suggestions, doings, and intentions have tremendous power.

- ["Honing Our Craft", Buddhadharma Magazine, Spring 2016,
  Ajahn Viradhammo]

Never underestimate the value of having a day job.

The Wholesome and the Unwholesome

Another formulation of Buddhist virtue is described by Sāriputta, one of the Buddha's two chief disciples. Sāriputta had a brilliant mind and a remarkable intellect. He is often credited with being the father of the Abhidhamma, the complex treatise on Buddhist psychology that was formulated after the time of the Buddha. In the discourse "Foremost" [AN 1.189] the Buddha described Sāriputta as being "the foremost of my bhikkhu disciples with great wisdom."

One of the charming details that comes from reading the Pāli Canon is how shy many of the Buddha's monks were in his presence. He would sometimes give them a brief discourse, and then disappear to his hut. The monks would then go to some other monk and ask for a more detailed explanation. Sāriputta was often the one to whom they went. Apparently even being foremost in wisdom is not as intimidating as being the Buddha.

In this particular case, however, Sāriputta was simply giving a teaching. The discourse is the "Sammādiṭṭhi Sutta: The Discourse on Right View" [MN 9]. It is one of the most complete expositions on right view in the Pāli Canon.

In his exposition of right view, Sāriputta explained how one way to describe right view is by understanding what is wholesome and what is unwholesome:

"When, friends, a noble disciple understands the unwholesome, the root of the unwholesome, the wholesome, and the root of the wholesome, in that way he is one of right view, whose view is straight, who has perfect confidence in the Dhamma, and has arrived at this true Dhamma."
- [MN 9.3]

Sāriputta went on to describe in detail what he meant by the unwholesome, giving us ten specific forms of unwholesome behavior:

"And what, friends, is the unwholesome, what is the root of the unwholesome, what is the wholesome, what is the root of the wholesome? (1) Killing living beings is unwholesome; (2) taking what is not given is unwholesome; (3) misconduct in sensual

pleasures is unwholesome; (4) false speech is unwholesome; (5) malicious speech is unwholesome; (6) harsh speech is unwholesome; (7) gossip is unwholesome; (8) covetousness is unwholesome; (9) ill will is unwholesome; (10) wrong view is unwholesome. This is called the unwholesome."
- [MN 9.4]

He continued by explaining that beneath each of these types of unwholesome action are unwholesome intentions, the motivations behind the unwholesome actions:

"And what is the root of the unwholesome? Greed is a root of the unwholesome; hate is a root of the unwholesome; delusion is a root of the unwholesome. This is called the root of the unwholesome."
- [MN 9.5]

Thus, being aware of our unwholesome actions becomes a gateway to awareness of the underlying problems, those of greed, hatred, and delusion. First we become aware of our unwholesome activities, but as our practice deepens we can see the intentions before they ever manifest as unwholesome activity.

It is also worth noting the tenth unwholesome activity, wrong view itself. This shows the importance of studying the Buddha's Dharma. This is not, of course, an end in itself, but a support mechanism for the whole of our practice.

In the Pāli Canon, the first collection in the Canon is the *Digha Nikāya: The Long Discourses of the Buddha*. And the very first discourse in the *Digha Nikāya* is the "Brahmajāla Sutta: What the Teaching is Not" [DN 1]. It lists 62 types of wrong view. It seems clear that the redactors of the Canon thought it was important to start the whole of the Canon with a list of things that the Buddha considered to be wrong view.

The Buddha's teachings are deep and subtle. This does not mean that they are inaccessible. But it does mean that you have to respect the depth and subtlety of his teachings. You have to be honest with yourself about when you do not understand something. Not understanding something is not a problem. Not understanding something and substituting something you just made up or you believe because of your conditioning is. This is a multi-pronged practice. In order to cultivate your mind in the way that the Buddha teaches, you must practice virtue, study the Dharma, and meditate. This is the path to awakening, and freedom from stress and suffering.

The Buddha saw holding wrong views and misrepresenting the Dharma as an activity that has grave consequences:

"These worthy beings who were ill conducted in body, speech, and mind, revilers of noble ones, wrong in their views, giving effect to wrong view in their actions, on the dissolution of the body, after death, have reappeared in a state of deprivation, in a bad destination, in perdition, even in hell;"
- [MN 51.25]

For those who misrepresent the Dharma, this is fair warning.

Sāriputta ended his teaching on the wholesome and the unwholesome in this way:

"When a noble disciple has thus understood the unwholesome, the root of the unwholesome, the wholesome, and the root of the wholesome, he entirely abandons the underlying tendency to lust, he abolishes the underlying tendency to aversion, he extirpates the underlying tendency to the view and conceit 'I am,' and by abandoning ignorance and arousing true knowledge he here and now makes an end of suffering. In that way too a noble disciple is one of right view, whose view is straight, who has perfect confidence in the Dhamma and has arrived at this true Dhamma."
- [MN 9.8]

It is particularly interesting that in this summary he points directly to the problems of greed, hatred, and delusion, and then goes into a discussion of "non-self." Non-self is one of the most misunderstood teachings of the Buddha. It is often taught as nihilism, a notion that the Buddha summarily rejected (in DN 1, as it happens). This is a good example of "wrong view."

(A discussion of non-self is beyond the framework of this Little Book, but a full discussion of non-self is in *The Little Book of Buddhist Wisdom.*)

In summary, another way to understand Buddhist virtue is by understanding and seeing what is wholesome and what is unwholesome. Remember that your thoughts are a type of action. It is particularly helpful to watch your thoughts, to evaluate them as being wholesome or unwholesome, abandon the unwholesome thoughts, and cultivate the wholesome ones.

Karma

Phenomena are preceded by the heart,
    ruled by the heart,
    made of the heart.
If you speak or act
with a corrupted heart,
then suffering follows you -
as the wheel of the cart,
the track of the ox
that pulls it.
Phenomena are preceded by the heart,
    ruled by the heart,
    made of the heart. If you speak or act
with a calm, bright heart,
then happiness follows you,
like a shadow that never leaves.
- [Dhp 1-2]

The religious schools of the Buddha's time had different understandings of karma. The Brahmins believed that you attained good karma by the correct performance of rituals. The Jains believe that karma consists of extremely fine and subtle matter that pollutes the soul, and it is through the practice of austerities that you free yourself from it. The Ājīvikas believed in unalterable destiny, or fate.

(The Jains still exist in India. The Ājīvikas went out of business in the early 2nd millennium.)

The Buddha's teaching on karma is that virtuous actions lead to good karma, and immoral actions lead to bad karma. It is one of the fundamental principles of the Buddha's teachings that our actions have results. Our future is not determined by a deity or higher power, nor is our future random. It is like the law of gravity, a natural force of nature.

Karma as Intention

Intention, I tell you, is kamma. Intending, one does kamma by way of body, speech, and mind.
- [AN 6.63]

34

The word "karma" literally means "action." However the Buddha also said that it is the intention behind the action that determines the karmic result. So an unskillful action does not have a negative result if the intention was skillful, (i.e., accidents happen). Conversely, a skillful action does not bring merit unless the intention was also skillful (i.e., accidents happen). The monastic code makes this clear:

The system of penalties the Buddha worked out for the rules is based on two principles. The first is that the training aims primarily at the development of the mind. Thus the factors of intention and perception often determine whether or not a particular action is an infringement of a rule. For instance, killing an animal accidentally is, in terms of the mind of the agent, very different from killing it purposefully, and does not count as an infringement of the rule against killing.

- [Ṭhānissaro Bhikkhu, "Introduction to the Patimokkha Rules"]

This does not mean that sloppy inattention gets you off the hook. What we are discussing is "skillful intention." This includes a) an altruistic motivation, b) wisdom, and c) appropriate attention. The brahma vihāras – loving-kindness, compassion, sympathetic joy, and equanimity - cultivate the first of these three qualities, right view coupled with reflection and discernment cultivates the second, and breath meditation cultivates the third.

We usually put our energy into "doing the right thing." There is nothing wrong with that; it is a noble effort. But we can get tied up in knots trying to reason out the ethical response to a situation. The Buddha suggested that we might be better served by working on our motivation.

Some years ago I was working in a very stressful environment, and I had an uncomfortable meeting with the head of my department. I had been thinking about skillful intention, and so during the meeting, I put my energy into thoughts of patience, kindness, and openness. I concentrated on conjuring up a wholesome state of mind and letting the results take care of themselves.

It was almost an out-of-body experience. I was able to respectfully acknowledge the other person while still standing my ground. What could have been an ugly scene had an optimal result. We aired our differences and no employees were injured.

So the first point to make about karma is that our actions have results. The second point is that the intention behind the action determines the result.

Karma as a Complex System

The third point about karma is that it is non-linear, and it is not deterministic. This is perhaps the most common misunderstanding about karma. When something goes wrong you will hear people say that it is due to their bad karma.

The results of our past actions are one factor in what happens in the present moment, but they are not the only one. What happens at any given time is the result of so many causes and conditions that the Buddha said that if you try to understand them all, you will go mad:

"The result of kamma is an inconceivable matter that one should not try to conceive; one who tries to conceive it would reap either madness or frustration."
- [AN 4.77]

A few years ago when a tsunami struck Asia, I heard a prominent Tibetan Lama say that the reason all those people died was because of their karma. This is a complete misunderstanding of why things happen. Earthquakes happen because tectonic plates move, not because everyone who lives near the fault line did something bad in a previous life.

Some people want the law of karma to be this way, to be deterministic and punitive, to be a doctrine of righteousness:

There are many people who would like the teaching of karma to be a theory of justice. People really would like the world be a just place. Karma is one way of getting justice out of the world, because it guarantees that the sucker will get his due sooner or later. The idea here is that there is a wonderful correlation that every action has a karmic result, or every result has a karmic source. If someone has stolen from you, or has done something terrible to you, as a result you have become poor by the end of your life, while the offender has become rich and dies rich. We would like to think that the offender will get his just punishment in the next life. That is the balance – the confirmation of justice is maintained by having a theory of multiple lifetimes in which everything works out eventually. But I don't think that the

Buddhist idea of karma was meant to be a form of justice. It is not supposed to explain everything and why everything is happening the way it is.

- [Gil Fronsdal, "Karma and Intention"]

Good things happen to bad people, and bad things happen to good people. Everyone has good and bad karma. An important factor is what karma manifests at a given time. This is why good people can have unhappy lives, and bad people can have good lives. In the "Mahākammavibhanga Sutta: The Greater Exposition of Action" [MN 136] the Buddha says this about karma and rebirth:

"Ānanda, there are four kinds of persons to be found existing in the world. What four? Here some person kills living beings, takes what is not given, misconducts himself in sensual pleasures, speaks falsehood, speaks maliciously, speaks harshly, gossips; he is covetous, has a mind of ill will, and holds wrong view. On the dissolution of the body, after death, he reappears in a state of deprivation, in an unhappy destination, in perdition, even in hell.

"But here some person kills living beings... and holds wrong view. On the dissolution of the body, after death, he reappears in a happy destination, even in the heavenly world.

"Here some person abstains from killing living beings, from taking what is not given, from misconduct in sensual pleasures, from false speech, from malicious speech, from harsh speech, from gossip; he is not covetous, his mind is without ill will, and he holds right view. On the dissolution of the body, after death, he reappears in a happy destination, even in the heavenly world.

"But here some person abstains from killing living beings... and he holds right view. On the dissolution of the body, after death, he reappears in a state of deprivation, in an unhappy destination, in perdition, even in hell."

- [MN 136]

Part of the Buddhist tradition is that the state of mind at death is extremely important in determining our next rebirth. If the mind is at ease when we die, the probability that good karma will manifest increases. If the mind is agitated when we die, the probability that negative karma will manifest increases.

Traditional Buddhists are particularly adamant about being allowed to die in peaceful circumstances. The consciousness is quite fragile at the time of death, and for some time afterwards, as people who have near-death experiences tell us. The usual time to wait for cremation is three days, although this varies by school. More importantly the area around the body should be free from negative energy. There should be no crying, sadness or hysteria. It is particularly auspicious to have a monk or nun preside over the death.

There is a famous story about Mahatma Gandhi and his death. Because of the political turmoil in India, Gandhi had a pretty good idea that he might be assassinated. But he was determined to die with love in his heart. He said, "If I am to die by the bullet of a madman, I must do so smiling. There must be no anger within me."

On January 30, 1948, Gandhi was fatally shot three times by a young man named "Nathuram Godse." Before he fell to the ground, Gandhi raised his hands to his face in the traditional Hindu greeting and bowed to Godse.

The Probabilistic Nature of Karma

So, you might ask, if what happens to us is the result of such complex conditions, why bother to cultivate virtue?

One reason is that while we cannot guarantee a wonderful future for ourselves, we can improve the odds. By cultivating generosity, kindness, love, compassion, wisdom, virtue, you will not only be a happier, more contented person, the chances of you having a happy future are greatly enhanced. You are playing the lottery with a lot of possible winning numbers.

The other reason is that even when we do something unskillful, the negative effect is dampened. The negative energy is absorbed and dissipated. The Buddha uses the analogy of a lump of salt to demonstrates this point:

"Here, bhikkhus, some person has created trifling bad kamma yet it leads him to hell, while some other person here has created exactly the same trifling kamma yet it is to be experienced in this very life, without even a slight [residue] being seen, much less abundant [residue].

"What kind of person creates trifling bad kamma that leads him to hell? Here, some person is undeveloped in body, virtuous

behavior, mind, and wisdom; he is limited and has a mean character, and he dwells in suffering. When such a person creates trifling bad kamma, it leads him to hell.

"What kind of person creates exactly the same trifling bad kamma and yet it is to be experienced in this very life, without even a slight [residue] being seen, much less abundant [residue]? Here, some person is developed in body, virtuous behavior, mind, and wisdom. He is unlimited and has a lofty character, and he dwells without measure. When such a person creates exactly the same trifling bad kamma, it is to be experienced in this very life, without even a slight [residue] being seen, much less abundant [residue].

"Suppose a man would drop a lump of salt into a small bowl of water. What do you think, bhikkhus? Would that lump of salt make the small quantity of water in the bowl salty and undrinkable?"

"Yes, lord."

"For what reason? Because the water in the bowl is limited, thus that lump of salt would make it salty and undrinkable.

"But suppose a man would drop a lump of salt into the river Ganges. What do you think, bhikkhus? Would that lump of salt make the river Ganges become salty and undrinkable?"

"No, Bhante."

"For what reason? Because the river Ganges contains a large volume of water, thus that lump of salt would not make it salty and undrinkable.

"So too, bhikkhus, some person here has created trifling bad kamma yet it leads him to hell, while some other person here has created exactly the same trifling kamma yet it is to be experienced in this very life, without even a slight [residue] being seen, much less abundant [residue]."
- [AN 3:100]

The greater our virtue, the greater our wisdom, and the greater our appropriate attention, the larger our "volume of water." The occasional indiscretion gets absorbed like a lump of salt in the Ganges.

There is a touching story in the Pāli Canon about King Pasenadi and his Queen Mallikā. Mallikā was a particularly virtuous, saintly person, and the King - despite the usual ups and downs of a royal marriage -

loved her dearly. But she had committed an act of sexual indiscretion, and then compounded it by lying to the King about it. When she died this weighed on her mind, and as a result she was reborn in one of the hell realms. However, because she was an otherwise virtuous person, she only spent seven days there, after which she was reborn in "the Tusita heaven."

While all this was happening, King Pasenadi, who was concerned about her welfare, asked the Buddha where she had been reborn. Out of compassion, the Buddha did not tell him. Also, King Pasenadi's faith in the Dharma was weak, so the Buddha did not want to discourage him. Thus, according to the story, the Buddha used his psychic powers to make King Pasenadi forget to ask the question.

After that seventh day, the Buddha went to King Pasenadi's palace for almsfood. The King finally remembered (!) to ask where the Queen was reborn. The Buddha told him that she was reborn in the Tusita heaven. The King was very pleased and said, "Where else could she be reborn? She was always thinking of doing good deeds. Venerable Sir! Now that she is gone, I, your humble disciple, hardly know what to do." In order to encourage the King in the Dharma, the Buddha told him:

> "Even royal chariots rot,
>   the body too does rot, decay,
> but undecaying's Dhamma of the Good
>   who to the good declare."
> - [Dhp 151]

(This story is not a discourse by the Buddha. It comes from the *Dhammapada-aṭṭhakathā*, which is a commentary on the Dhammapada. The reference is iii, 119-123. But whether it is true or not, it's still a good story. Internet search: "buddhist women mallika")

So the odds of a favorable result improve in two ways. One is that we simply have more good karma, so good karma is more likely to manifest. The other reason is that even when bad karma does manifest, our river of virtue absorbs it.

Choice

So far we have discussed past karma. But there is also present karma, the choices we make in the present moment.

Your state of mind influences the experience of the present moment. Someone cuts you off in traffic. That is simply an event. The next issue is what state of heart and mind do you bring to the experience? Are you tired and frustrated and angry? That will manifest in one way. Are you calm and tranquil and happy? That will manifest in another way.

One purpose of meditation is to cultivate a mind that is more skillful, more altruistic and wiser, calmer and more serene, and that affects what manifests in the present moment. Two people can have the same experience and have two different responses to that experience. And the same person can have a different response to the same set of conditions depending on their state of mind in the present moment.

This makes it possible to intervene in the present moment and modify the result. A skillful action with a skillful intention makes it possible to create a positive outcome even if negative karma is manifesting.

An extreme example of this was Angulimala. Angulimala was a serial killer who became an arahant. If unwholesome karma always manifested as an unwholesome result, if it was deterministic, it would not have been possible for Angulimala to become enlightened. He would have had to suffer the consequences of his actions first [MN 86].

To be sure, Angulimala did not get off the hook entirely. People knew who he was, and they used to throw things at him when he went on alms rounds. But being an arahant is a better outcome than being reborn in hell.

A trained mind exercises choice. It is an empowered mind. An untrained mind does not exercise choice. It acts on impulse. One of the things that we are doing by training the mind is we are asserting control over it. We are subduing the Nazis running around in our heads:

There was a period of time in my Buddhist practice where I became very good at... learning how to just be with things, and just let go of everything else. I would just let go and let go and just be really present. That can be very peaceful, and life could be very peaceful, very content, and very happy just being present by letting go. That was quite fine when I was a monk since I did not have to make a lot of choices. Then I became a parent, and just letting go and being present was not going to be enough. Lying in bed at two o'clock in the morning when the kid has an earache, or the two kids are fighting. Just let go, let go - this is not enough. You have to make a choice about how to act. You have to be creative and think ahead. A lot of thought has to go into how to respond to this situation. You cannot just sit there and be present to this situation. Being present and letting go is very important, but there is more to it. Something is required of us.

So what do we do about that part of life when something is required of us? Buddha's teachings about karma have a lot to do with this aspect of our lives, the places where we have choice, and how we make choices. The practice of mindfulness brings us to that place where we see that we have a choice.

- [Gil Fronsdal, "Karma and Intention"]

You don't have to believe an abstract theory on karma and you do not have to believe in rebirth; you will see it work in this lifetime. A mind that is cultivating virtue is evolving toward greater joy, greater happiness, and less suffering. You may need a little faith in the process, but eventually you will reap the fruits of skillful intentions. You do not need to wait until some future life. You do not even have to believe that there will be a future life. A heart that is open, warm, kind, loving, wise, and at peace with itself is its own reward.

The End of Karma

You may have surmised by now that there are limits to what good karma can bring you. All unenlightened beings have mixed karma, and bad karma can always manifest. And the physical forces of the universe play their part. There are always those pesky tectonic plates moving about. Conditioned existence is very risky and full of dangers.

The Buddha was after something better than simply improving the odds. And according to the Buddha's teaching, as beings are born and reborn into different realms, even skillful beings eventually fall into bad habits. They become proud. They become vain. They become pleased with themselves, and oops, there you go, sliding down the karmic chain. They inevitably end up in an unhappy place. This dance has been going on throughout limitless lifetimes.

On the night of his awakening, therefore, he kept looking. He did not just want to acquire good karma; he wanted it to end. He wanted to free himself from the uncertainties of conditioned existence.

This is a radical notion. Now, the path to ending karma runs through the process of first developing good karma. So don't think that everything that we are doing is for naught. This is a journey of a thousand miles. You can't skip steps. That is why there are books on meditation called *Breath by Breath* and *With Each and Every Breath*. It is one breath at a time. It is one moment at a time. And progress is not linear. It is steps forward and back and forward and back. It requires patience and persistence.

But out there over the horizon is this intriguing notion that we can stop creating karma altogether. We can free ourselves from the uncertainties of conditioned existence. We can guarantee our happiness, and we can end our suffering:

"Bhikkhus, there are these four kinds of kamma proclaimed by me after I realized them for myself with direct knowledge. What four? There is dark kamma with dark result; there is bright kamma with bright result; there is dark-and-bright kamma with dark-and-bright result; and there is kamma that is neither dark nor bright with neither-dark-nor-bright result, kamma that leads to the destruction of kamma. These are the four kinds of kamma proclaimed by me after I realized them for myself with direct knowledge."
- [AN 4.232]

It is this fourth kind of karma, karma that leads to the destruction of karma, that the Buddha was looking for and ultimately found on his extraordinary spiritual journey.

In summary, these are the key points about the Buddha's teaching on karma:

1. The law of karma is a process of cause and effect, actions and their results.
2. The quality of our intentions determines the karmic result.
3. Karma is a complex system, non-linear and not deterministic.
4. Karma works on probabilities, and the more good karma we have the better our odds of having a favorable result. A developed, skillful mind absorbs and dissipates the effects of occasional unskillful actions.
5. We can affect the results of past karma by training our minds to make skillful choices in the present moment.
6. The ultimate goal is to end the creation of karma completely.

The Ten Perfections

There is one final formulation of Buddhist virtue, and that is the "pāramīs" (Sanskrit: pāramitā). Technically in Pāli it is the "dasa pāramiyo," the "Ten Perfections."

While some traditionalists assert that the Ten Perfections are part of the Buddha's original teachings, it seems clear that they are a later formulation. This is not to denigrate them. Just because something came later does not mean that it is not in the letter and the spirit of what the Buddha taught.

The Buddha's teachings are extremely pragmatic. He was not trying to teach a system of philosophy or explain life, the universe and everything. He was trying to help us solve our fundamental problems of living, to show us a way of living more skillfully, more happily, and eventually to become free from stress and suffering altogether.

To that extent it would be missing the elephant in the room to quibble over a teaching's historical legacy, rather than its usefulness in obtaining freedom. The Buddha on his deathbed said this about any teaching:

"But where on such comparison and review they [the teachings] *are found to conform to the suttas and the discipline, then the conclusion must be: 'Assuredly this is the word of the Buddha, it has been rightly understood by this monk.'"*
- [DN 16.4.11]

Thus the true test of any teaching is that it conforms to the whole of the suttas and the monastic code.

The ten pāramīs are qualities derived from the Buddha's teaching and are formulated in a particular way. (In the Mahāyāna traditions of China, Tibet, etc. there are only six pāramīs.)

There is a particularly charming aspect to the pāramīs in that they are closely related to the Jātaka tales, folk stories of the Buddha's previous lives. The Jātaka tales were probably formulated around the same time as the pāramīs, in the first century or two after the Buddha died, and are probably adaptations of Indian folk stories. In each Jātaka the Buddha-in-training – the "Bodhisatta" (Sanskrit: Bodhisattva) - appears as an animal, a god, a human, etc., and each story emphasizes one or more of the Perfections.

In the centuries that followed, more Buddhists probably learned about the Buddha's teachings from Jātaka tales than from any other source. Buddhist temples throughout Asia depict one or more Jātakas in stone reliefs. At the Mahathupa ("Great Stupa") in Sri Lanka, all 550 Jātaka tales are represented inside of the reliquary chamber. There are even "Jātaka stupas" in India that mark the location at which a Jātaka story took place.

The pāramīs, then, coupled with the Jātaka tales, provide a unique way to learn about the conduct that is expected of a disciple of the Buddha. It is the cultivation of these qualities that makes one a disciple of the Buddha, not adherence to a creed.

The ten perfections are:

1. generosity (Pāli: dāna)
2. moral conduct (Pāli: sīla)
3. renunciation (Pāli: nekkhamma)
4. wisdom (Pāli: pañña)
5. energy (Pāli: viriya)
6. patience (Pāli: khanti)
7. honesty (Pāli: sacca)
8. resolve (Pāli: adhiṭṭhāna)
9. loving-kindness (Pāli: mettā)
10. equanimity (Pāli: upekkhā)

We have already discussed most of these, but in the spirit of the pāramīs and the Jātaka tales, let's look at a Jātaka story associated with each Perfection

1. Generosity

Moral: Have no fear when doing wholesome deeds.

Once upon a time, there was a very rich man living in Benares, in northern India. When his father died, he inherited even more wealth. He thought, "Why should I use this treasure for myself alone? Let my fellow beings also benefit from these riches."

So he built dining halls at the four gates of the city - north, east, south and west. In these halls he gave food freely to all who wished it. He became famous for his generosity. It also became known that he and his followers were practitioners of the Five Training Steps [Precepts].

In those days, there was a Silent Buddha meditating in the forest near Benares. He was called "Buddha" because he was enlightened.

Being enlightened, he was filled with compassion and sympathy for the unhappiness of all beings. So he wished to teach and help them to be enlightened just as he was. But the time of our story was a most unfortunate time, a very sad time. It was a time when no one else was able to understand the Truth, and experience life as it really is. And since this Buddha knew this, that was why he was silent.

While meditating in the forest, the Silent Buddha entered into a very high mental state. His concentration was so great that he remained in one position for seven days and nights, without eating or drinking.

When he returned to the ordinary state, he was in danger of dying from starvation. At the usual time of day, he went to collect alms food at the mansion of the rich man of Benares.

When the rich man had just sat down to have lunch, he saw the Silent Buddha coming with his alms bowl. He rose from his seat respectfully. He told his servant to go and give alms to him.

Meanwhile, Māra, the god of death, had been watching. Māra is the one who is filled with greed for power over all beings. He can only have this power because of the fear of death.

Since a Buddha lives life fully in each moment, he has no desire for future life, and no fear of future death. Therefore, since Māra could have no power over the Silent Buddha, he wished to destroy him. When he saw that he was near death from starvation, he knew that he had a good chance of succeeding.

Before the servant could place the food in the Silent Buddha's alms bowl, Māra caused a deep pit of red hot burning coals to appear between them. It seemed like the entrance to a hell world.

When he saw this, the servant was frightened to death. He ran back to his master. The rich man asked him why he returned without giving the alms food. He replied, "My lord, there is a deep pit full of red hot burning coals just in front of the Silent Buddha."

The rich man thought, "This man must be seeing things!" So he sent another servant with alms food. He also was frightened by the same pit of fiery coals. Several servants were sent, but all returned frightened to death.

Then the master thought, "There is no doubt that Māra, the god of death, must be trying to prevent my wholesome deed of giving alms food to the Silent Buddha. Because wholesome deeds are the beginning of the path to enlightenment, this Māra wishes to stop me at all costs. But he does not understand my confidence in the Silent Buddha and my determination to give."

So he himself took the alms food to the Silent Buddha. He too saw the flames rising from the fiery pit. Then he looked up and saw the terrible god of death, floating above in the sky. He asked, "Who are you?" Māra replied, "I am the god of death!"

"Did you create this pit of fire?" asked the man.

"I did," said the god.

"Why did you do so?"

"To keep you from giving alms food, and in this way to cause the Silent Buddha to die! Also to prevent your wholesome deed from helping you on the path to enlightenment, so you will remain in my power!"

The rich man of Benares said, "Oh Māra, god of death, the evil one, you cannot kill the Silent Buddha, and you cannot prevent my wholesome giving! Let us see whose determination is stronger!"

Then he looked across the raging pit of fire, and said to the calm and gentle Enlightened One, "Oh Silent Buddha, let the light of Truth continue to shine as an example to us. Accept this gift of life!"

So saying, he forgot himself entirely, and in that moment there was no fear of death. As he stepped into the burning pit, he felt himself being lifted up by a beautiful cool lotus blossom. The pollen from this miraculous flower spread into the air, and covered him with the glowing color of gold. While standing in the heart of the lotus, the rich man of Benares poured the alms food into the bowl of the Silent Buddha. Māra, god of death, was defeated!

In appreciation for this wonderful gift, the Silent Buddha raised his hand in blessing. The rich man bowed in homage, joining his hands above his head. Then the Silent Buddha departed from

Benares, and went to the Himalayan forests. Still standing on the wonderful lotus, glowing with the color of gold, the generous master taught his followers. He told them that practicing the Five Training Steps is necessary to purify the mind. He told them that with such a pure mind, there is great merit in giving alms - indeed it is truly the gift of life!

When he had finished teaching, the fiery pit and the lovely cool lotus completely disappeared.

- [Jātaka 40, *The Silent Buddha*]

This story references a "Silent Buddha." In Pāli this is "Pacceka Buddha" (Sanskrit: Pratyekabuddha). A Pacceka Buddha is a Buddha who decides not to teach, usually because he does not think that anyone will understand the Dharma. For example, if a Buddha awakens in Nazi Germany, circumstances may not be conducive to hearing and practicing the Dharma.

2. Moral conduct

A priest, who was maintained by the King of Kosala, had sought the Three Refuges; he kept the Five Commandments, and was versed in the Three Vedas. "This is a good man," thought the King, and showed him great honor.

But the priest thought to himself, "The King shows honor to me beyond other brahmins, and has manifested his great regard by making me his spiritual director. But is his favor due to my goodness or only to my birth, lineage, family, country and accomplishments? I must clear this up without delay."

Accordingly, one day when he was leaving the palace, he took unbidden a coin from a treasurer's counter, and went his way. Such was the treasurer's veneration for the brahmin that he sat perfectly still and said not a word.

Next day the brahmin took two coins, but still the official made no remonstrance.

The third day the brahmin took a whole handful of coins. "This is the third day," cried the treasurer, "that you have robbed his Majesty," and he shouted out three times, "I have caught the thief who robs the treasury."

In rushed a crowd of people from every side, crying, "Ah, you've long been posing as a model of goodness." And dealing him two or three blows, they led him before the King.

In great sorrow the King said to him, "What led you, brahmin, to do so wicked a thing?" And he gave orders, saying, "Off with him to punishment."

"I am no thief, sire," said the brahmin.

"Then why did you take money from the treasury?"

"Because you showed me such great honor, sire, and because I made up my mind to find out whether that honor was paid to my birth and the like or only to my goodness. That was my motive, and now I know for certain that it was my goodness and not my birth and other advantages, that won me your majesty's favor. Goodness I know to be the chief and supreme good. I know too that to goodness I can never attain in this life, while I remain a layman, living in the midst of sinful pleasures. Wherefore, this very day I would fain go to the Master at Jetavana [monastery]

and renounce the world and become a monk. Grant me your leave, sire."

The King consenting, the brahmin set out for Jetavana. His friends and relations in a body tried to turn him from his purpose, but finding their efforts of no avail, left him alone. He came to the Master and asked to be admitted to the Saṅgha. After admission to the lower and higher orders, he won by application spiritual insight and became an arahant, whereon he drew near to the Master, saying, "Sir, my joining the Order has borne the Supreme Fruit," thereby signifying that he had won Arahatship.

- [Jātaka 86, The Virtue Experiment]

3. Renunciation

Once upon a time in Mithilā in the realm of Videha there was a King named Makhādeva, who was righteous and ruled righteously. For successive periods of eighty-four thousand years he had respectively amused himself as prince, ruled as viceroy, and reined as King. All these long years had he lived, when one day he said to his barber, "Tell me, friend barber, when you see any grey hairs in my head."

So one day, years and years after, the barber did find among the raven locks of the King a single grey hair, and he told the King so.

"Pull it out, my friend," said the King, "and lay it in my palm."

The barber accordingly plucked the hair out with his golden tongs, and laid it in the King's hand. The King had at that time still eighty-four thousand years more to live, but nevertheless at the sight of that one grey hair he was filled with deep emotion. He seemed to see the King of Death standing over him, or to be cooped within a blazing but of leaves.

"Foolish Makhādeva!" he cried. "Grey hairs have come upon you before you have been able to rid yourself of defilements." And as he thought and thought about the appearance of his grey hair, he grew aflame within. The sweat rolled down from his body, while his raiment oppressed him and seemed intolerable.

"This very day," he thought, I will renounce the world for the life of a spiritual seeker."

To his barber he gave the grant of a village, which yielded a hundred thousand pieces of money. He sent for his eldest son and said to him, "My son, grey hairs are come upon me, and I have become old. I have had my fill of human joys, and fain would taste the joys divine. The time for my renunciation has come. Take the sovereignty upon yourself. As for me, I will take up my abode in the pleasure garden called Makhādeva's Mango-grove, and there tread the ascetic's path."

As he was thus bent on leading the seeker's life, his ministers drew near and said, "What is the reason, sire, why you adopt the seeker's life?"

Taking the grey hair in his hand, the King repeated this stanza to his ministers:

> "Lo, these grey hairs that on my head appear
> Are Death's own messengers that come to rob
> My life. 'Tis time I turned from worldly things,
> And in the hermit's path sought saving peace."

And after these words, he renounced his sovereignty that self-same day and became a recluse. Dwelling in that very Mango-grove of Makhādeva, he fostered the Four Perfect States within himself, and, dying with insight full and unbroken, was reborn in the Realm of Brahma. Passing thence, he became a King again in Mithilā, under the name of Nimi, and after uniting his scattered family, once more became a hermit in that same Mango-grove, winning the Four Perfect States and passing thence once more to the Realm of Brahma.

- [Jātaka 9, *King Makhādeva*]

It is worth saying something additional about renunciation. We usually think of renunciation as giving up something that we want. We make a sacrifice in order to get something that we think will be better. And there is certainly that aspect to renunciation.

Ṭhānissaro Bhikkhu tells the following story. It is from a book that was written by a friend of his:

"I've told you the story about the Chinese woman teaching her stepdaughter, while they were playing chess, that if you want to be happy in life you have to decide that there's one thing you want more than anything else, and you have to be willing to sacrifice everything else for that one thing. That, of course, was a lesson the stepdaughter didn't want to hear. What she did notice though, was that her stepmother was losing chess pieces all over the board. So she decided, "Well, here's my chance to beat my stepmother in chess." She started playing more aggressively, but it turned out to be a trap. The stepmother had been sacrificing her pieces strategically to lure the girl in, and then she checkmated her.

"Of course, the way the stepmother played chess was an illustration of the principle she was trying to teach. If you're willing to sacrifice some pawns and knights and other pieces here and there, you can win. That's how we should live our lives, realizing we can't keep all our pawns and win at the same time. We have to make our choices. There are a lot of either/ors in life. We prefer the both/and — and sometimes not just the both/and. We want the both/and/and/and/and/and...

"But if you really want to have something to show for your life, you've got to recognize where it's strictly either/or. You've got to decide that there are important qualities in the mind that have to take top priority over everything else."

- [Ṭhānissaro Bhikkhu, "Perfections as Priorities"]

That is one kind of renunciation. We give up a lesser happiness for a greater one.

But another way to think of renunciation is that what we are giving up is the stress and struggle that come with a conventional, worldly life. We want to have nice things: clothes, a house, good food, an attractive companion, and so forth. And in order to get those things, we have to work. We have to manage our money. We have to fix the car and maintain the house. We have families and sometimes complicated relationships. Families can be wonderful at times, but they can also bring a lot of drama. Then there is our health and managing that.

It is not that these things are all bad all the time. Of course, they are not. But any complication brings with it some burdens.

When monks and nuns ordain, in the Buddhist tradition that is called "homeleaving." Monks and nuns are also sometimes called "renunciates." They leave the worldly life behind. They leave their biological families and enter the family of the Saṅgha. It is a process of extreme simplification. And in doing so, they not only leave behind worldly pleasures, they leave behind all the stress and struggle that comes with it.

So a different way to think of renunciation is that you are giving up that kind of ultimately futile stress, struggle, and suffering. And even in the lay world you can practice renunciation. You can simplify your life. You can minimize your entanglements. Ṭhānissaro Bhikkhu uses the phrase "helping people without becoming entangled with them." You can consume less. You can learn to be happy with worldly things or be happy without them. You can enjoy a good meal or you can skip a few meals. You don't have to give up worldly pleasures. What you give up is the clinging and the craving, and you also give up the stress and suffering that goes with them.

4. Wisdom

Once on a time when Brahmadatta was reigning in Benares, the Bodhisatta came to life again as a monkey. When full-grown, he was as big as a mare's foal and enormously strong. He lived alone on the banks of a river. In the middle of the river was an island where mangoes and bread-fruits, and other fruit trees grew.

In mid-stream, half way between the island and the river bank, a solitary rock rose out of the water. Being as strong as an elephant, the Bodhisatta used to leap from the bank on to this rock and then on to the island. Here he would eat his fill of the fruits that grew on the island, returning at evening by the way he came. And such was his life from day to day.

Now there lived in those days in that river a crocodile and his mate. She, being with young, was led by the sight of the Bodhisatta journeying to and fro to conceive a longing for the monkey's heart to eat. So she begged her lord to catch the monkey for her. Promising her that he would do this, the crocodile went off and crawled onto the rock, meaning to catch the monkey on his evening journey home.

After ranging about the island all day, the Bodhisatta looked out at evening towards the rock and wondered why the rock stood so high out of the water. For the story goes that the Bodhisatta always marked the exact height of the water in the river, and of the rock in the water. So, when he saw that, though the water stood at the same level, the rock seemed to stand higher out of the water. He suspected that a crocodile might be lurking there to catch him. In order to find out if that was true, he shouted, as though addressing the rock, "Hi! Rock!" And, as no reply came back, he shouted three times, "Hi! Rock!" And as the rock still kept silence, the monkey called out, "Why is it, friend rock, that you won't answer me to-day?"

"Oh!" thought the crocodile, "So the rock is in the habit of answering the monkey. I must answer for the rock to-day."

Accordingly, he shouted, "Yes, monkey, what is it?"

"Who are you?" said the Bodhisatta.

"I'm a crocodile."

"What are you sitting on that rock for?"

"To catch you and eat your heart."

As there was no other way back, the only thing to be done was to outwit the crocodile. So the Bodhisatta cried out, "There's no help for it then but to give myself up to you. Open your mouth and catch me when I jump."

Now you must know that when crocodiles open their mouths, their eyes shut. So, when this crocodile unsuspiciously opened his mouth, his eyes shut. And there he waited with closed eyes and open jaws! Seeing this, the wily monkey made a jump on to the crocodile's head, and thence, with a spring like lightning, leaped to the bank. When the cleverness of this feat dawned on the crocodile, he said, "Monkey, he that in this world possesses the four virtues overcomes his foes. And I think that you possess all four." And, so saying, he repeated this stanza:

> Who so, o monkey king, like you, combines
> Truth, foresight, fixed resolve, and fearlessness,
> Shall see his routed foemen turn and flee.

And with this praise of the Bodhisatta, the crocodile went back to his own dwelling place.

- [Jātaka 54, The Heart of the Monkey]

The four virtues are lovingkindness (mettā), compassion (karuṇā), empathetic joy (muditā), and wisdom (paññā).

5. Energy

Once upon a time when Brahmadatta was king in Benares, in Kāsi the Bodhisatta was born into a trader's family. When he was grown up, he used to travel about trading with 500 carts. On one occasion he came to a sandy wilderness sixty leagues across, the sand of which was so fine that, when grasped, it slipped through the fingers of the closed fist. As soon as the sun got up, it grew as hot as a bed of charcoal-embers and nobody could walk upon it.

Accordingly, those traversing it used to take firewood, water, oil, rice and so forth on their carts, and only travelled by night. At dawn they used to range their carts in a circle to form a fort, with an awning spread overhead, and after an early meal used to sit in the shade all the day long. When the sun went down, they had their evening meal, and as soon as the ground became cool, they used to yoke their carts and move forward.

Travelling on this desert was like voyaging over the sea. A "desert-pilot" as he was called, had to convoy them over by knowledge of the stars. And this was the way in which our merchant was now travelling that wilderness.

When he had only some seven more miles before him, he thought to himself, "Tonight will see us out of this sandy wilderness." So, after they had had their supper, he ordered the wood and water to be thrown away, and yoking his carts, set out on the road. In the front cart sat the pilot upon a couch looking up to the stars in the heavens and directing the course thereby.

But he had been so long without sleep that he was tired, and he fell asleep. As a result he did not see that the oxen had turned round and were retracing their steps. All night the oxen kept on their way, but at dawn the pilot woke up, and, observing the disposition of the stars overhead, shouted out, "Turn the carts round! Turn the carts round!" And as they turned the carts round and were forming them into line, the day broke.

"Why this is where we camped yesterday," cried the people of the caravan. "All our wood and water is gone, and we are lost." So saying, they unyoked their carts and made a fort and spread the awning overhead; then each man flung himself down in despair beneath his own cart.

The Bodhisatta thought to himself, "If I give in, every single one will perish." So he ranged to and fro while it was still early and cool, until he came on a clump of kusa-grass. "This grass," he thought, "can only have grown up here thanks to the presence of water underneath." So he ordered a spade to be brought and a hole to be dug at that spot.

They dug down 90 feet until the spade struck a rock, and everybody lost heart. But the Bodhisatta, feeling sure there must be water under that rock, descended into the hole and took his stand upon the rock. Stooping down, he applied his ear to it, and listened. Catching the sound of water flowing beneath, he came *out and said to a serving-lad, "My boy, if you give in, we shall all perish. So take heart and courage. Go down into the hole with this iron sledge-hammer, and strike the rock."*

Obedient to his master's bidding, the lad, resolute where all others had lost heart, went down and struck the rock. The rock which had dammed the stream, split apart and fell in. Up rose the water in the hole till it was as high as a palm-tree, and everybody drank and bathed. Then they chopped up their spare axles and yokes and other surplus gear, cooked their rice and ate it, and fed their oxen. And as soon as the sun set, they hoisted a flag by the side of the well and travelled on to their destination. There they bartered away their goods for twice and four times their value. With the proceeds they returned to their own home, where they lived out their term of life and in the end passed away to fare thereafter according to their deserts. The Bodhisatta too,

after a life spent in charity and other good works, passed away likewise to fare according to his deserts.

- [Jātaka 2, *The Sandy Road*]

This story emphasizes energy as diligence and persistence. But the Buddha also taught the "Four Right Strivings," which he defined as Right Energy in the Noble Eightfold Path. These are:

1. Make an effort, arouse energy, apply your mind, and strive for the nonarising of unarisen evil unwholesome states.

2. Make an effort, arouse energy, apply your mind, and strive for the abandoning of arisen evil unwholesome states.

3. Make an effort, arouse energy, apply your mind, and strive for the arising of unarisen wholesome states.

4. Make an effort, arouse energy, apply your mind, and strive for the "maintenance of arisen wholesome states."

6. Patience

When my children were young, I bought a lovely rendering of this story called "The Magic of Patience." It was one of their favorite books. It is still in print and is published by Dharma Publishing. If you have children I highly recommend it.

Despite countless lifetimes of selfless and virtuous action, perhaps due to the ripening of karma from ancient and forgotten misdeeds, the Bodhisatta was once born in a low state as a large buffalo. Yet even in this brute animal state where ignorance prevails, he treated all who he encountered with compassion.

With a grim appearance and always caked with mud, the buffalo was quite intimidating. One malicious monkey however, aware of the buffalo's natural goodness, was not afraid and liked nothing more than to tease him. The monkey knew that the buffalo would be forgiving and not take action against him. The monkey would climb on the buffalo and swing from his horns, stand at his feet and keep him from grazing when hungry, and would even poke the buffalo's ears with a sharp stick. The monkey would mount the buffalo's back and ride him, holding a stick in his hand like the Lord of Death. It is said that the wicked consistently walk the path opposed to discipline, while the good-hearted, due to their practice of virtue, patiently aim to benefit even the wicked.

One day a tree spirit saw the monkey riding that buffalo and was scandalized by the indignities being heaped upon the great being. He wanted to know why the buffalo would not defend himself from such torture. The tree spirit appeared in the path of the two and told the buffalo that he would easily be able to kill the monkey if he chose to and asked him why he had not done so already. Did he not know his own strength? Was he the monkey's slave? Did the monkey win him in a game of chance? Was he for some reason afraid of the monkey? Was he not aware the monkey was wicked? The buffalo replied that none of these were the case, and the fact that the monkey was devious, unstable, and powerless was actually the reason he put up with him. He wanted to help the monkey.

The buffalo said that it is easy to be patient with those who are more powerful, but when enduring injuries from the powerless, it is an opportunity to show real patience and virtue, however uncomfortable it may be. This satisfied the tree spirit who then threw the monkey from the buffalo's back, taught the buffalo a protective charm and vanished.

- [Jātakamala 33, The Patient Buffalo]

7. Honesty

Once upon a time, the King of Benares went on a picnic in the forest. The beautiful flowers and trees and fruits made him very happy. As he was enjoying their beauty, he slowly went deeper and deeper into the forest. Before long, he became separated from his companions and realized that he was all alone.

Then he heard the sweet voice of a young woman. She was singing as she collected firewood. To keep from being afraid of being alone in the forest, the King followed the sound of the lovely voice. When he finally came upon the singer of the songs, he saw that she was a beautiful fair young woman, and immediately fell in love with her. They became very friendly, and the King became the father of the firewood woman's child.

Later, he explained how he had gotten lost in the forest, and convinced her that he was indeed the King of Benares. She gave him directions for getting back to his palace. The King gave her his valuable signet ring, and said, "If you give birth to a baby girl, sell this ring and use the money to bring her up well. If our child turns out to be a baby boy, bring him to me along with this ring for recognition." So saying, he departed for Benares.

In the fullness of time, the firewood woman gave birth to a cute little baby boy. Being a simple shy woman, she was afraid to take him to the fancy court in Benares, but she saved the King's signet ring.

In a few years, the baby grew into a little boy. When he played with the other children in the village, they teased him and mistreated him, and even started fights with him. It was because his mother was not married that the other children picked on him. They yelled at him, "No-father! No-father! Your name should be No-father!"

Of course this made the little boy feel ashamed and hurt and sad. He often ran home crying to his mother. One day, he told her how the other children called him, "No-father! No-father! Your name should be No-father!" Then his mother said, "Don't be ashamed, my son. You are not just an ordinary little boy. Your father is the King of Benares!"

The little boy was very surprised. He asked his mother, "Do you have any proof of this?" So she told him about his father giving her the signet ring, and that if the baby was a boy she should bring him to Benares, along with the ring as proof. The little boy said, "Let's go then." Because of what happened, she agreed, and the next day they set out for Benares.

When they arrived at the King's palace, the gate keeper told the King the firewood woman and her little son wanted to see him. They went into the royal assembly hall, which was filled with the King's ministers and advisers. The woman reminded the King of their time together in the forest. Finally she said, "Your majesty, here is your son."

The King was ashamed in front of all the ladies and gentlemen of his court. So, even though he knew the woman spoke the truth, he said, "He is not my son!" Then the lovely young mother showed the signet ring as proof.

Again the King was ashamed and denied the truth, saying, "It is not my ring!"

Then the poor woman thought to herself, "I have no witness and no evidence to prove what I say. I have only my faith in the power of truth." So she said to the King, "If I throw this little boy up into the air, if he truly is your son, may he remain in the air without falling. If he is not your son, may he fall to the floor and die!"

Suddenly, she grabbed the boy by his foot and threw him up into the air. Lo and behold, the boy sat in the cross-legged position, suspended in mid-air, without falling. Everyone was astonished, to say the least! Remaining in the air, the little boy spoke to the mighty King. "My lord, I am indeed a son born to you. You take care of many people who are not related to you. You even maintain countless elephants, horses and other animals. And yet, you do not think of looking after and raising me, your own son. Please do take care of me and my mother."

Hearing this, the King's pride was overcome. He was humbled by the truth of the little boy's powerful words. He held out his arms and said, "Come to me my son, and I will take good care of you."

Amazed by such a wonder, all the others in the court put out their arms. They too asked the floating little boy to come to them. But he went directly from mid-air into his father's arms. With his son seated on his lap, the King announced that he would be the crown prince, and his mother would be the number one queen.

In this way, the King and all his court learned the power of truth. Benares became known as a place of honest justice. In time the King died. The grownup crown prince wanted to show the people that all deserve respect, regardless of birth. So he had himself crowned under the official name, "King No-father!" He went on to rule the Kingdom in a generous and righteous way.

- [Jātaka 7, *Prince No-father*]

8. Resolve

Candādevī, wife of the King of Kāsi, had, to her great grief, no son. Sakka's throne was heated by her piety, and he persuaded the Bodhisatta, then in the Tāvatiṃsa heaven, to be born as her son. The Bodhisatta reluctantly agreed. Great were the rejoicings over his birth. He was called "Temiya" because on the day of his birth. There was a great shower throughout the kingdom and he was born wet.

When he was one month old, he was brought to the King, and, as he lay in his lap, he heard grievous sentences passed on some robbers brought before the King. Later, as he lay in bed, Temiya recollected his past births and remembered how he had once reigned for twenty years as King of Bārāṇasī, and, as a result had suffered in Ussada hell (niraya) for twenty thousand years. Anguish seized him at the thought of having to be King once more, but the goddess of his parasol, who had once been his mother, consoled him by advising him to pretend to be dumb and incapable of any action.

He took this advice, and for sixteen years the King and Queen, in consultation with the ministers and others, tried every conceivable means of breaking his resolve, knowing him to be normal in body. However, all their attempts failed, and at last he was put in a chariot and sent with the royal charioteer, Sunanda, to the charnel ground, where he was to be clubbed to death and buried.

At the Queen's urgent request, however, Temiya was appointed to rule over Kāsi for one week before being put to death. But the enjoyment of royal power did not weaken his resolve. The charioteer, under the influence of Sakka, took Temiya to what he considered to be the charnel-ground and there, while Sunanda was digging the grave, Temiya stole up behind him and confided to him his purpose and his resolve to lead the holy life. Sunanda was so impressed by Temiya's words that he immediately wished to become a spiritual seeker himself, but Temiya wanted him to inform his parents of what had happened.

When the King and Queen heard Sunanda's news, they went with all their retinue to Temiya's hermitage and there, after hearing Temiya teach, they all became spiritual seekers. The inhabitants of the three kingdoms adjacent to Bārāṇasī followed their example, and great was the number of ascetics. Sakka and Vissakamma provided shelter for them. Crowds flocked together there and were called the "Mūgapakkha samāgama."

- [Jātaka 538, The Story of Temiya, the Dumb Cripple]

There is a mention of a "goddess of parasol" in the story. This is a protector deity. As you can see, she was once the Bodhisatta's mother.

Sakka is the ruler of the "Tāvatiṃsa heaven" (Sanskrit: Trāyastriṃśa). "Tāvatiṃsa" means "heaven of the 33 devas" (gods/goddesses). It is the second heaven above the human realm in the Buddhist cosmology. This heaven shows up frequently in the Buddhist stories. One instance is where the Bodhisatta's birth mother, Maya, was reborn when she died just one week after his birth.

Vissakamma is one of the deities in the Tāvatiṃsa heaven.

If all of this Buddhist cosmology freaks you out, do not worry about it. As I found out on my trip to India, the distinction between myth and reality there is quite blurred. If this is a problem for you, just go along for the ride, and put the cosmological references on the back burner of your mind for now. For a full treatment of the Buddhist cosmology see *The Little Book on Buddhist Rebirth*.

The Jātaka tales sometimes remind me of the Fractured Fairy Tales from Rocky and Bullwinkle. Have fun with them. Don't worry; be happy.

9. Loving-kindness

Once two hunters, chiefs of villages, made a pact that if their children happened to be of different sexes, they should marry each other. One had a boy called "Dukūlaka," because he was born in a wrapping of fine cloth. The other had a daughter called "Pārikā," because she was born beyond the river.

When they grew up the parents married them, but because they had both come from the Brahma world, they agreed not to consummate the marriage. With their parent's consent they became spiritual seekers and lived in a hermitage provided for them by the god on the banks of the Migasammatā River.

One day Sakka foresaw that a danger threatened them. "They will lose their sight." So he went to Dukūlaka, and having sat on one side, after saluting him he said, "Sir, I foresee a danger which threatens you. You must have a son to take care of you. Follow the way of the world."

Dukūlaka replied, "O Sakka, why do you say such a thing? Even when we lived in a house we abstained from sexual intercourse. Can we practice it now when we have come into the forest and are living a life withdrawn from the world?"

"Well, if you will not do as I say, then at the proper season touch Pārikā's navel with your hand."

This he promised to do, and Sakka, after saluting him, returned to his own abode. Then Dukūlaka told the matter to Pārikā, and at the proper time he touched her navel with his hand. Then the Bodhisatta descended from the heavenly world and entered her womb and was conceived there.

When the son was born, they called him "Sāma," and, because he was of golden color, he came to be called "Suvaṇṇasāma."

One day, after Sāma was grown up, his parents, returning from collecting roots and fruits in the forest, took shelter under a tree on an anthill. The water that dripped from their bodies angered a snake living in the anthill, and his venomous breath blinded them both. When it grew late, Sāma went in search of them and brought them home. From then onwards he looked after them.

Now at that time a king named "Piliyakkha" reigned in Benares. He, in his great desire for venison, had entrusted the kingdom to his mother, and armed with the five kinds of weapons had come into the region of Himavat. While there he had gone on killing deer and eating their flesh until he came to the river Migasammatā. At last he reached the spot where Sāma used to come and draw water. Seeing the footsteps of deer, he erected his shelter with boughs of the color of gems, and taking his bow and fitting a poisoned arrow on the string he lay there in ambush. In the evening the Bodhisatta, having collected his fruits and put them in the hermitage, made his salutation to his parents, saying, "I will bathe and go and fetch some water." He took his pot, and surrounded by his train of deer went to the bathing-place.

The King in his shelter saw him coming, and said to himself, "All the time that I have been wandering here I have never seen a man before. Is he a god or a nāga [a deity in the form of a snake]? Now if I go up and ask him, he will fly up into heaven if he is a god, and he will sink into the earth if he is a nāga. But I shall not always live here in Himavat, and one day I shall go back to Benares. My ministers will ask me whether I have not seen some new marvel in the course of my rambles in Himavat. If I tell them that I have seen such and such a creature, and they proceed to ask me what its name was, they will blame me if I have to answer that I do not know. So I will wound it and disable it, and then ask it."

In the meantime, the animals went down first and drank the water and came up from the bathing-place, and then the Bodhisatta went slowly down into the water like a great elder who was perfectly versed in the rules, and, being intent on obtaining absolute calm, put on his bark garment and threw his deer-skin on one shoulder and, lifting up his water-jar, filled it and set it on his left shoulder. At this moment the King, seeing that it was the time to shoot, let fly a poisoned arrow and wounded the

Bodhisatta in the right side, and the arrow went out at the left side.

The Bodhisatta thought, "I have no enemies in this district of Himavat, and I have no enmity against anyone." As he said these words, blood poured out of his mouth and, without seeing the King, he addressed this stanza to him:

"Who, as I filled my water-jar, has from his ambush wounded me,

"Brahmin or Khattiya, Vessa, who can my unknown assailant be?"

Then he added another stanza to show the worthlessness of his flesh as food:

"You cannot take my flesh for food, you cannot turn to use my skin,

"Why would you think me worth your aim? What was the gain thou thought to win?"

When the King heard this, he thought to himself, "Though he has fallen wounded by my poisoned arrow, he neither reviles me nor blames me. He speaks to me gently as if soothing my heart. I will go up to him." So he went and stood near him, saying:

"I of the Kāsis am the lord, King Piliyakkha named, and here,

"Leaving my throne for greed of flesh, I roam to hunt the forest deer.

"Skilled in the archer's craft am I, stout is my heart nor given to change;

"No Nāga can escape my shaft if once he comes within my range."

Thus, praising his own merits, he proceeded to ask the other man his name and family:

"But who are you? Whose son are you? What is your name? Tell me your name,

"Your father's name and family, tell me your father's and thine own."

The Bodhisatta replied:

"They called me 'Sāma' while I lived, an outcast hunter's son am I.

"But here stretched out upon the ground in woeful plight you see me lie.

"Pierced by that poisoned shaft of thine, I lie helpless like any deer,

"The victim of your fatal skill, bathed in my blood I wallow here.

"Thy shaft has pierced my body through, I vomit blood with every breath,

"Yet, faint and weak, I ask thee still, why did you seek my death?

"You cannot take my flesh for food, you cannot turn to use my skin.

"Why did you think me worth thy aim? What was the gain you thought to win?"

When the King heard this, he did not tell the real truth, but made up a false story and said:

"A deer had come within my range, I thought that it would be my prize,

"But seeing you it fled in fright. I had no angry thought for you."

Then the Bodhisatta replied, "Why do you say that, O King? In all this Himavat there is not a deer which flies when he sees me."

When the King heard him, he thought to himself, "I have wounded this innocent being and told a lie. I will now confess the truth." So he said:

"Sāma, I did not see a dear. Why should I tell a needless lie?

"I was overcome by wrath and greed and shot that arrow. It was I."

Then he thought again, "Suvaṇṇasāma cannot be dwelling alone in this forest, his relations no doubt live here; I will ask him about them." So he uttered a stanza:

"Why did you come here this morning, friend? Who told you to take your water-jar

"And fill it from the river's bank and bear the burden back so far?"

When he heard this, the Bodhisatta felt a great pang and uttered a stanza, as the blood poured from his mouth:

"My parents live In yonder wood, blind and dependent on my care,

"For their sakes to the river's bank I came to fill my water-jar."

Then he went on, telling the King of his parents' condition, and how overwhelmed by grief they will be when he does not return.

The King, on hearing about the parents, thought to himself, "This man has been fostering his parents in his excessive piety and devotion to duty, and even now amidst all his pain he only thinks of them, I have done evil to such a holy being. How can I comfort him? I will watch over his father and mother as he watched over them." Then said, "I will protect and foster them as you have done till now."

The Bodhisatta replied, "It is well, O King, then do foster them." So he pointed out the way to his parents to him.

The King accepted the trust, and the Bodhisatta, having thus delivered his final message, became unconscious.

The King thought he was dead. But a goddess, Bahusodarī, who had been Sāma's mother seven births earlier, lived in Gandhamādana and kept constant watch over him. This day she had gone to an assembly of the gods and had forgotten him for a while, but she suddenly became aware of the danger into which he had fallen. She stood in the air near Piliyakkha, and ordered the King to go and tell Sāma's parents what had happened. He did as he was commanded, and, having revealed his identity, gradually informed them of Sāma's fate and his own part in it. But neither Dukūlaka nor Pārikā spoke to him one word of resentment. They merely asked to be taken to where Sāma's body lay. Arriving there, Pārikā made a solemn Act of Truth (saccakiriyā), and the poison left Sāma's body, making him well.

Bahusodarī did likewise in Gandhamādana, and Sāma's parents regained their sight. Then Sāma preached to the marveling King, telling him how even the gods take care of those who cherish their parents.

The story was told (by the Buddha) in reference to a young man of Sāvatthī. Having heard the Buddha preach, the young man obtained his parents' leave with great difficulty and joined the Order. For five years he lived in the monastery, and, failing to attain insight, he returned to the forest and strove for twelve years more. His parents grew old, and as there was no one to look after them, their retainers robbed them of their goods. Their son, hearing of this from a monk who visited him in the forest, at once left his hermitage and returned to Sāvatthī. There he tended his parents, giving them food and clothing which he acquired by begging, often starving himself that they might eat. Other monks blamed him for supporting lay folk, and the matter was reported to the Buddha. But the Buddha, hearing his story, praised him and told this story of The Good Son.

- [Jātaka 540, *The Good Son*]

This story is longer than the others, and unusually long for a Jātaka. And while the language of the translation is somewhat stylized, it is still one of my favorites. The selflessness and lack of animosity of both the Good Son and his parents is very inspiring.

In the Canon, the Jātaka stories begin and end with a "story in the present." This is the context in which the Buddha supposedly told the story. I have left these out in the other cases, but here I added the ending part of the "story in the present" at the end. We all do good things for which we are criticized. Here we see the Buddha recognizing the noble intention of a disrobed monk, defending him in the face of such criticism.

10. Equanimity

The quality of equanimity may not be obvious in the following story. However, in the Buddhist tradition the last ten Jātaka stories came to be associated with the Perfections, this one being the tenth. The equanimity in the story is that of Narada, the great Brahma, who descended from heaven to convince King Angati that he held a wrong view, about the perniciousness of that wrong view, and the benefits of leading a virtuous life.

In the Kingdom of Videha, there lived King Angati and his beautiful daughter, Ruja. Ruja was his greatest joy, for though he had sixteen thousand wives, she was his only child. Upon her he lavished his wealth, sending her baskets of flowers, delicate trinkets, and garments of spun gold and silver. He even entrusted to her the honor of distributing every two weeks a thousand pieces of gold to the poor and sickly. This almsgiving won him the love of his people and the admiration of his daughter.

On the eve of the great festival of the full moon, King Angati, freshly bathed and dressed, stood with his three chief advisers surveying from his terrace the white city beneath him. As the streets gleamed with the rays of the advancing moon, the King turned to his counselors and asked, "How best shall we amuse ourselves on this festival eve?"

The first one, General Alata, suggested conquering new lands. The second, who was in charge of the King's diversions, thought only of feasting and dancing. The third, the chief court brahmin, knew of a naked ascetic living in the forest just outside the city, and felt that it would be most entertaining to go seek out his advice. Since King Angati had always enjoyed listening to ascetics, he agreed to the brahmin's suggestion.

Thus the royal chariot, made of solid ivory, was polished and covered with silver ornaments for the King's nocturnal journey. White were the four swift horses that drew it, white was the seven-tiered umbrella, white the royal fan. From a distance, the King in his shining chariot could have been a shaft of moonlight.

As he and his entourage approached the center of the forest, they saw a crowd surrounding a naked man seated on the ground and knew this must be Guna the ascetic. Not wanting to disturb the gathering, the King alighted from the chariot and greeted Guna on foot. After exchanging respectful words with him, King Angati seated himself at one side on a small mat covered with squirrel skins and told Guna the purpose of his visit. "The festival of the full moon is upon us," he said, "and we have come to ask you to remove some doubts from our minds."

He then proceeded to ask him the rules of right behavior toward parents and teachers, wives and children, brahmins and the aged, the army and his people, adding, "And most important, we should like to know how it is that some men go to hell while others find their way to heaven."

Now, it happened that at that time and in that land there was no true sage to whom men could turn for advice, and by default Guna, though merely an ignorant ascetic, childish and given to half-truths, had gained a reputation for wisdom. Thus when Guna seized this occasion to recite his heretical theories, many people believed him. He spoke in this way: "There is no right or wrong way to behave. Whatever you do, whether it be virtuous or evil, has no effect on your future, for your life is arranged in advance of your birth [predestined]. Whether a man thrusts his sword into his enemy's heart or whether he gives alms is irrelevant to a life over which we have no control. Hell? Heaven? Nonsense! There is no other world than this. So follow your own will and seek your own pleasure."

After Guna had finished his shocking speech, General Alata was the first to speak. "That confirms what I have always felt, for in a former birth I was a hunter, killing sacred cows and committing many wrongs. And yet do you see me suffer in this life? I am a prosperous general and have never been sent to hell."

Then a slave dressed in rags tearfully related how he had always been and still was a virtuous man, never failing to give alms in previous lives. "But look upon me now," he said, "a prostitute's son, with hardly enough to eat, and still I give half of my food away to those as hungry as I, and still I keep the fast days. But my past and present virtues go unheeded, alas!"

King Angati, swayed by the stories he heard, spoke of his own unfailing devotion to almsgiving, but still he was not satisfied, saying, "Though I have not suffered as a result of my good deeds, I have not had a bit of enjoyment from them either." And *convinced of the truth of Guna's words, he abruptly turned from the ascetic and, without saluting him, departed.*

From then on, he resolved to make no further effort to do good. He relinquished all cares and unpleasant kingly duties to his advisers. He no longer made decisions. He busied himself only with watching others at work and at play. Since nothing he did was to have any consequences, he reasoned, he would have no more to do with the business of life. Worst of all, he stopped giving alms.

A month passed, and his subjects lamented the loss of their King's interest in them. Ruja wept for her father, for she heard the mourning of his unhappy people and saw him harden his heart and close his ears to reason.

On the next festival of the full moon, Ruja dressed herself in her finest garments, gifts from her father, and entered his court. When he inquired how she was enjoying life, she answered that she lacked only one thing. She explained: "Tomorrow, my father, is the sacred fifteenth day. Please order, if you will, your courtiers to bring me a thousand pieces of gold that I may bestow them at once upon the people, as has been your custom."

Her father replied indifferently, "Alms? Give away our gold? I have no wish to carry on such a foolish custom. Destiny makes us what we are. For what reason should I waste my wealth? Please do not annoy me further with such inconsequential matters, my daughter."

Ruja realized with horror that her father had truly strayed from the holy precepts. She pleaded with him thus: "O my father, I have heard that he who listens to fools himself becomes a fool and that he who lets himself be led by children himself becomes a child. I fear that Guna's words have turned you into such a person. As for your prosperous General Alata, he is merely reaping the good from past acts of merit, but it will soon be used up and he will go straight to hell. The beggar who ranted to you of his sufferings must be making up for some grave misdemeanor in his past and will soon come to the end of his misery. The good he is doing now, along with his accumulated merit, will bring him to know the joys of heaven."

Then Ruja related how she herself, seven births ago, was born as a blacksmith's son who, with his wicked friends, used to corrupt other men's wives. As a result, in succeeding lives Ruja had been born as a castrated goat, a monkey whose father had cruelly removed his son's testicles, a eunuch, and other mutilated beings. Though the King still loved his daughter, he was unmoved by her arguments and refused to budge from his fixed opinions.

Ruja then stepped to one side of the court, knelt down, and with her hands together above her head, made reverences in ten directions to the highest deities, those in the Brahma heavens, begging them to give some sign which would shock her father out of his heresy.

At that moment the Bodhisatta, whose name was Narada and who was the Great Brahma of that time, was looking earthward from his seat in his heaven. He happened to hear Ruja's supplications and decided to help her. Before taking the journey to earth, he thought to himself, "There is none other than I who can drive away false doctrines. I shall go to the King in some unusual garb so that first my appearance and then my words will arrest his attention. King Angati values ascetics. I will dress like the most striking of them, and when he sees me, he will listen well."

The Great Brahma dressed according to his word, in a red-mottled garment with a black antelope skin over one shoulder. He carried a golden pole on his shoulders from which two golden begging bowls were suspended by strings of pearls. His hair was matted as is the custom of ascetics, but with a golden needle tucked inside. Thus arrayed, he sped through the sky like the moon when the clouds race past it on a windy night, and stood suspended in the air before the King and his court. Ruja, who had returned to the King's side, immediately recognized the Brahma and bowed down to pay reverence to him. But the King, alarmed by the heavenly presence, rushed down from his throne to cry, "Who are you? From where do you come?"

Narada answered in this solemn way: "I am the Great Brahma from the Brahma heavens. I have come to tell you, King Angati, that you are condemning yourself to hell."

"I say there is no heaven or hell," Angati boasted. "To prove it, lend me five hundred pieces of gold, and if I am wrong, I will return one thousand pieces to you from hell when I am there."

Narada warned him in this way: "If you were a virtuous man, I would gladly lend you gold, for it is not hard to collect a debt from a man in heaven. But men like you, denying the precepts, following false doctrines, are bound for hell, and when you hear what I will tell you about hell, you will see that no one would dare collect a debt from a man in such a place. There is not just one hell, but a thousand hells. Animals of all sizes will chew on your skin and bite at your bones. Flocks of ravens, crows, and vultures will prey upon you. Dogs with iron teeth will tear at your entrails. Hot winds, razor-edged mountains, burning coals, and sword-leafed trees will torture you."

At last Angati was moved and trembled with fear. He looked to the Bodhisatta for help and asked him humbly how he could uncloud his mind and regain his senses. Narada then told him that while he was King and in good health, he should assume the responsibilities of his realm, providing for the poor, the hungry, the aged, and the brahmins. "Let your mind guide your body, making you a sure but self-restrained man," he said. "Only then will you find the path to heaven. Let your daughter teach you, for she has learned the right way."

King Angati begged forgiveness and, with his daughter, bowed in reverence and gratitude to the Bodhisatta, who then turned and sped back to the Brahma world.

- [Jātaka 544, *Narada, The Great Brahma*]

This story has many notable features. First of all, it is an ascetic who holds a wrong view who starts all the trouble. This points to the Buddha's many cautions about the abuse of religious authority. It also points to a regular theme of his teaching, and that is that wrong view brings with it particularly dire consequences.

Another interesting feature is something that can be particularly problematic for Western audiences, and that is his graphic description of the hell realms. But this is also a consistent theme of his teaching, that unwholesome intentions and unwholesome actions have an unwholesome result now or in the future, and that future may be in a hell realm.

One of the most endearing parts of this story is the pivotal role of King Angati's daughter Ruja, who shows great love and compassion for her father, and great wisdom as well. It is her skill and her virtue that show the way to the proper path, and it is her deep compassion for him that causes Narada to descend from heaven in order to convince King Angati of the error of his ways. And it is Narada's mastery of equanimity that enables Narada to debate successfully with the King in a calm and reasoned way.

Altogether this is a rich story with important lessons about the responsibilities of having power and the benefits of living virtuously.

Postscript

Recently I had dinner with some friends, and one of them was complaining about people who get assistance from government programs like Welfare and WIC (the food program for Women, Infants and Children). When she finished I simply responded, "That doesn't bother me in the least." I don't know who was more surprised, she or I. I went on to say something about bailing out Wall Street and how much was spent on the last two wars. "In America we have capitalism for the poor, and socialism for the rich," I quoted. [Michael Harrington, *The Other America*]

What I was really thinking, however, was that a mind that is upset about people on Welfare, people who are at the very bottom of the economic food chain, is not a happy mind.

The world is the way it is. That doesn't mean that we sit idly by and do nothing. What we do is assess what we can do in the face of a problem. If the answer is something, then we do that. If the answer is nothing, then we do that. Either way there is no use getting upset about it.

In the movie "Bridge of Spies" attorney James Donovan marvels at his client Rudolph Abel, who was accused of being a Soviet spy, and his lack of worry. "Would it help?" said Abel.

I recently stumbled across an article called "Is this the world's happiest man?" It is about Matthieu Ricard, a Tibetan Buddhism monk. Ricard was originally trained as a molecular biologist, receiving his Ph.D. From the Pasteur Institute in 1972. But in a journey not unlike the Buddha's, he found that "success" in this worldly way is limited.

More recently Ricard has been the subject of a number of brain studies, including one at the University of Wisconsin:

Neuroscientist Richard Davidson wired up the monk's [Ricard] skull with 256 sensors at the University of Wisconsin as part of research on hundreds of advanced practitioners of meditation.

The scans showed that when meditating on compassion, Ricard's brain produces a level of gamma waves - those linked to consciousness, attention, learning and memory - 'never reported before in the neuroscience literature', Davidson said.

The scans also showed excessive activity in his brain's left prefrontal cortex compared to its right counterpart, giving him an abnormally large capacity for happiness and a reduced propensity towards negativity, researchers believe.

- [Claire Bates, The Daily Mail, Feb. 14, 2016, "Is this the world's happiest man?"]

As to his "secret," Ricard gives some advice, among which is:

Develop a cluster of positive inner qualities.

There is no happiness center in the brain. Happiness results from a certain number of basic human qualities, says Ricard. He calls it a "flourishing" of good qualities like compassion and empathy.

"It's an inner freedom," he says. "Freedom from animosity, freedom from greed, freedom from craving — all those toxins that poison your own happiness and that of others."

- [Gina Vivinetto, Today, Dec. 3, 2015, "Secrets of kindness from Matthieu Ricard, the 'world's happiest man'"]

In becoming happy, in becoming virtuous, you become an anti-body in a poisonous world.

Cultivating virtue is not just following some rules. It is about cultivating a wholesome state of mind. The Dalai Lama famously says, "My religion is kindness." Without kindness, compassion, patience, understanding, and wisdom, without virtue, the rest of this practice and the rest of life itself is almost meaningless. If you only do one thing in your life, cultivate virtue.

The scent of virtue
  Is unsurpassed
Even by sandalwood, rosebay,
  Water lily, and jasmine.
- [Dhp 55]

Appendices

Appendix A - Glossary of Terms

Abhidhamma (Pāli, Sanskrit: Abhidharma)

The *Abhidhamma* is the third of the "three baskets" in the Pāli Canon, although scholars date it to 100 to 200 years after the time of the Buddha. It has been variously described as philosophy, psychology, and metaphysics. The *Abhidhamma* is highly revered in the Theravada tradition, and highly criticized in the others (!).

Ajahn (also Ajaan)

Thai word meaning "teacher." In Buddhism it is a monk who has at least ten years of seniority.

Aṅguttara Nikāya

Literally "Increased by One Collection," but usually translated as "Numerical Discourses." It is the second of the five *nikāyas*, or collections, in the Sutta Pitaka of the Pāli Canon. The Aṅguttara Nikāya is organized in eleven books according to the number of items referenced in them (i.e., the Four Noble Truths is in the Book of Fours).

arahant (Pāli, Sanskrit: arahat)

Literally "one who is worthy," a perfected person, i.e., one who has attained nirvāṇa.

awakening

Also called "enlightenment." It is a sudden insight into transcendent, ultimate truth. This is the goal of the Buddha's system of training. After awakening one is free from unnecessary suffering, and after death is free from all suffering. In Buddhist cosmology a fully awakened person, or "arahant," is free from the rounds of rebirth.

Bhante (Pāli)

Literally "Venerable Sir." Although it is a masculine term, it is gender neutral and is used for both monks and nuns.

bhikkhu (Pāli, Sanskrit: bhikṣu)

Literally "beggar." An ordained Buddhist monk. However the term can also refer to anyone following the Buddhist path. When the Buddha gave a talk he would address it to the highest ranking persons there. The rank order was 1) monks, 2) nuns, 3) lay men, and 4) lay women. Thus if even one monk were present, he would address the talk to "bhikkhus."

Bodhisatta (Pāli, Sanskrit: Bodhisattva)
The term used by the Buddha to refer to himself both in his previous lives and as a young man in his current life, prior to his enlightenment, in the period during which he was working towards his own liberation.

deva
In the Buddhist cosmology, devas are gods or heavenly beings that live in the realm just above humans.

Dharma (Sanskrit, Pāli: dhamma)
In Buddhism, the word "dharma" has three different meanings. The first meaning is the universal nature of how things are. At the time of the Buddha, each religious school had its own Dharma, or understanding of how things are. The second meaning of Dharma is the teachings of the Buddha. The third meaning is phenomena. Buddhism sees everything in terms of causes and effects. Mental activities, for example, are dharmas. When referring to the teachings of the Buddha, the word Dharma is capitalized. When referring to phenomena, it is not capitalized.

Dhammapada-aṭṭhakathā ("aṭṭhakathā" is Pāli for *explanation, commentary*)
Commentary to the Dhammapada.

Digha Nikāya
The Long Discourses of the Buddha (Pāli digha = "long"). It is the first of the five *nikāyas*, or collections, in the Sutta Pitaka of the Pāli Canon. Pāli scholar Joy Manné makes the argument that the Digha Nikāya was particularly intended to make converts (Bhikkhu Bodhi pointedly refers to this as "for the purpose of propaganda"!), with its high proportion of debates and devotional material.

Eight Precepts
These are lay precepts for people who want to practice more intensively. They are often observed on Uposatha Days. The additional precepts (to the Five Precepts) are: 1) refrain from eating after noon, 2) refraining from entertainment, wearing jewelry or using perfumes, and 3) sleeping on luxurious beds or over-sleeping.

fetters
Literally a "chain" that shackles one to the rounds of rebirth. The fetters are 1) self-identity view, 2) attachment to rites and rituals, 3) doubt, 4) sense desire, 5) ill will 6) desire for material existence, 7) desire for immaterial existence 8) conceit, 9) restlessness, and 10) ignorance.

Five Faculties

Also called the "Five Strengths" or the "Five Spiritual Faculties." They are 1) faith, 2) energy (vigor/diligence), 3) mindfulness, 4) concentration, and 5) wisdom.

Four Foundations of Mindfulness

Also called the Four Establishings of Mindfulness, and the Four Frames of Reference. The Four Foundations of Mindfulness are 1) the body, 2) feelings, or "feeling tones," 3) mental formations, and 4) mental phenomena.

jhāna (Pāli, Sanskrit: dhyāna)

"meditative absorption." The jhānas are states of high concentration. In the final formulation there are four "material" jhānas and four "immaterial" jhānas.

kōan (Japanese, also *kung-an*)

A kōan is a riddle or puzzle that Zen Buddhists use during meditation to help them unravel a greater truth and break through conceptual thinking.

Majjhima Nikāya

The Middle Length Discourses of the Buddha. It is the second of the five *nikāyas*, or collections, in the Sutta Pitaka of the Pāli Canon. It is generally believed to be the most important collection of discourses in the Canon. The *Majjhima Nikāya* corresponds to the *Madhyama Āgama* which survives in two Chinese translations. Fragments also exist in Sanskrit and Tibetan.

Māra (Pāli, Sanskrit)

Literally "bringer of death." Māra is a deity who embodies the ability of experience, especially sensory experience, to seduce and trap the mind, particularly to prevent the cessation of suffering.

nibbāna (Pāli, Sanskrit: nirvāṇa)

Nibbāna is one of the terms that is used to define the goal of the Buddhist path. It literally means "to extinguish," and means to extinguish the three flames of greed, hatred, and delusion.

non-returner (Pāli, Sanskrit: anāgāmi)

The third of four stages of awakening. A non-returner eliminates the fourth and fifth "fetters" – sense craving and ill-will – and will become an arahant with no more rebirths in the material realm.

once-returner (Pāli: sakadāgāmin, Sanskrit: sakṛdāmin)

The second of four stages of awakening. A once-returner has weakened the fourth and fifth "fetters" – sense craving and ill-will – and will become an arahant with no more than one more rebirth in the material realm.

Pāli Canon

The Pāli Canon is the collection of Buddhist texts preserved in the Pāli language. It consists of three *Pitakas*, or "baskets." These are the *Vinaya Pitaka* (the monastic code), the *Sutta Pitaka* (the discourses of the Buddha and his senior disciples), and the *Abhidhamma Pitaka*, a later work that is variously described as Buddhist philosophy, psychology and metaphysics. The *Abhidhamma Pitaka* is unique to Theravada, or southern, Buddhism; the other collections have versions in the Chinese and Tibetan Canons.

parinibbāna (Pāli, Sanskrit: parinirvāna)

Literally "nibbāna after death." When the body of an arahant dies, this frees the being from samsara, the rounds of rebirth.

Pātimokkha (Pāli, Sanskrit: Prātimoksa)

Literally "towards liberation." It is the list of monastic rules in the Vinaya.

Sangha (Pāli, Sanskrit: samgha)

Literally "community." At the time of the Buddha the term Sangha referred either to the community of monastics (monks and nuns) or the noble Sangha, which is the community of people who are stream-enterers, once-returners, non-returners, and arahants.

Satipatthāna (Pāli)

The "Four Foundations of Mindfulness": (1) the body, (2), feelings/sensations, (3) mental formations (thoughts and emotions), and (4) *dharmas*, or phenomena.

Samana (Pāli, Sanskrit: Śramana)

A wandering ascetic.

Samyutta Nikāya

The Connected Discourses. It is the third of the five *nikāyas*, or collections, in the Sutta Pitaka of the Pāli Canon. The *Samyutta Nikāya* consists of fifty-six chapters, each governed by a unifying theme that binds together the Buddha's suttas or discourses.

Seven Factors of Awakening (enlightenment)

(1) Mindfulness, (2) investigation, (3) energy, (4) joy/rapture, (5) tranquility, (6) concentration, and (7) equanimity.

stream-entry (Pāli: sotāpanna, Sanskrit: srotāpanna)

The first of four stages of awakening. A stream-enterer overcomes the first three "fetters" – self view, attachment to rites and rituals, and skeptical doubt – and will become an arahant in no more than seven lifetimes with no rebirths in the lower realms.

sutta (Pāli, Sanskrit: sutra)
A discourse of the Buddha or one of his disciples. The Pāli word "sutta" refers specifically to the Pāli Canon. The words "sutta" and the Sanskrit form "sutra" literally mean "thread," and are related to the English word "suture."

Tathāgata (Pāli, Sanskrit)
A word the Buddha used when referring to himself. It's literal meaning is ambiguous. It can mean either "thus gone" (tathā-gata) or "thus come" (tathā-āgata). It is probably intentionally ambiguous, meaning that the Buddha, having attained a final awakening, was beyond all comings and goings.

Upāsaka (masculine), **Upāsikā** (feminine) (Pāli, Sanskrit)
Literally "attendant." A lay follower of the Buddha, one who has taken and keeps the Five Precepts.

Uposatha (Pāli, Sanskrit: Upavasatha)
Traditionally held on the new moon and full moon days of the lunar month. This is the day when monastics gather to recite the Pātimokkha (monastic rules) and confess any transgressions. Lay people observe either the Five Precepts or, if they spend the day at a temple or monastery, the Eight Precepts.

Visuddhimagga (Pāli)
Literally, *The Path of Purification*. The *Visuddhimagga* is a Theravada commentarial work attributed to the monk Buddhaghosa, who formulated it in Sri Lanka in the fifth century CE.

Appendix B - Bibliography

Allen, Charles, *The Search for the Buddha*, New York: Carroll & Graf Publishers, 2002, 2003.

Bhikkhu Bodhi (Translator), *The Connected Discourses of the Buddha: A Translation of the Saṃyutta Nikāya*, Somerville: Wisdom Publications, 2003.

Bhikkhu Bodhi (Translator), *The Numerical Discourses of the Buddha: A Translation of the Aṅguttara Nikāya*, Somerville: Wisdom Publications, 2012.

Bhikkhu Bodhi, Bhikkhu Khantipalo, Hecker, Hellmuth, Ireland, John D., Norman, K.R., Olendzki, Andrew, Rhys Davids, C.A.F., Sister Khema, *Thera-Therīgāthā: Verses of Arahant Bhikkhus and Bhikkhunīs*, Kandy: Buddhist Publication Society, 2012.

Bhikkhu Ñāṇamoli (Translator), Bhikkhu Bodhi (Translator), *The Middle Length Discourses of the Buddha: A Translation of the Majjhima Nikāya (Teachings of the Buddha)*, Somerville: Wisdom Publications, 1995.

Chalmers (Translator), E.B. Cowell (ed.), *The Jataka, Vol. I*, Cambridge: University Press, 1895.

Dalai Lama, Thupten Jinpa (Translator), *The Middle Way: Faith Grounded in Reason*, Somerville: Wisdom Publications, 2009.

Eiseley, Loren, *The Unexpected Universe*, New York: Mariner Books, 1972.

Francis, H. T. (Translator), E.B. Cowell (ed.), *The Jataka, Vol. III*, Cambridge: University Press, 1897.

Francis, H. T. (Translator), E.B. Cowell (ed.), *The Jataka, Vol. V*, Cambridge: University Press, 1905.

Fronsdal, Gil, *The Dhammapada: A New Translation of the Buddhist Classic with Annotations*, Boston & London: Shambhala, 2011.

Goldberg, Natalie, *The Great Failure: My Unexpected Path to Truth*, San Francisco: HarperOne, 2005.

Kelly, John (translator), *Milindapañha: The Questions of King Milinda*, Access to Insight (Legacy Edition), http://www.accesstoinsight.org/tipitaka/kn/miln/miln.intro.kell.html, 2013.

Rosenberg, Larry, *Breath by Breath: The Liberating Practice of Insight Meditation*, Boston: Shambhala, 2004.

Rouse, W. H. D. (Translator), E.B. Cowell (ed.), *The Jataka, Vol. II*, Cambridge: University Press, 1895.

Rouse, W. H. D. (Translator), E.B. Cowell (ed.), *The Jataka, Vol. IV*, Cambridge: University Press, 1901.

Rouse, W. H. D. (Translator), E.B. Cowell (ed.), *The Jataka, Vol. VI*, Cambridge: University Press, 1907.

Salzberg, Sharon, *Lovingkindness: The Revolutionary Art of Happiness*, Boston: Shambhala, 2002.

Shaw, Sarah, *The Jātakas: Birth Stories of the Bodhisatta*, London: Penguin Books, 2006.

Ṭhānissaro Bhikkhu, *Selves & Not-self: The Buddhist Teaching on Anatta*, Valley Center: Metta Forest Monastery, 2011.

Ṭhānissaro Bhikkhu, *The Buddhist Monastic Code*, Valley Center: Metta Forest Monastery, 2013.

Ṭhānissaro Bhikkhu, *The Wings to Awakening*, Valley Center: Metta Forest Monastery, 2010.

Ṭhānissaro Bhikkhu, *Udana: Exclamations*, Valley Center: Metta Forest Monastery, 2014.

Ṭhānissaro Bhikkhu, *With Each and Every Breath*, Valley Center: Metta Forest Monastery, 2013.

Thich Nhat Hanh, Kornfield, Jack, at al, *For a Future to be Possible*, Berkeley: Parallax Press, 1993.

Walsh, Maurice (Translator), *The Long Discourses of the Buddha: A Translation of the Digha Nikāya (Teachings of the Buddha)*, Somerville: Wisdom Publications, 1995.

White, Rosalyn, *The Magic of Patience*, Cazadero: Dharma Publishing, 2009.

57432178R00058

Made in the USA
San Bernardino, CA
19 November 2017